There's An Egg in My Soup

Tom Galvin went to Poland in 1994 to work with APSO, the State body for overseas aid, and worked and lived in a Polish State school for five years. He later worked as a journalist for the *Warsaw Voice* and Radio Polonia in Warsaw. On his return in 1999, he worked as a staff writer for the old *In Dublin* magazine (without the ads), becoming editor until 2003. In 2004 he worked with Vincent Browne's *Village* magazine, as arts and culture editor, and later as a feature writer and photographer. He now works for the *Evening Herald*, on the *Polski Herald* supplement and as books editor. He has written two books for the tourist market, *The Little Book of Dublin* (2004) and *That's Cork* (2005). He lives in Wicklow with his Polish wife, Asha.
www.tomgalvin.com

There's an Egg in my Soup...

and other adventures of an Irishman in Poland

TOM GALVIN

THE O'BRIEN PRESS
DUBLIN

First published 2007 by The O'Brien Press Ltd,
12 Terenure Road East, Dublin 6, Ireland.
Tel: +353 1 4923333; Fax: +353 1 4922777
E-mail: books@obrien.ie
Website: www.obrien.ie

ISBN: 978-1-84717-048-4

British Library Cataloguing in Publication Data
Galvin, Tom
There's an egg in my soup : an Irish man in Poland
1. Galvin, Tom - Homes and haunts - Poland 2. Irish - Poland 3. Teachers - Poland
4. Poland - Description and travel 5. Poland - Social life and customs
I. Title
943.8'057'092

1 2 3 4 5 6 7 8 9 10
07 08 09 10 11 12

Editing, typesetting, layout and design: The O'Brien Press Ltd
Printing: Cox and Wyman Ltd.

To Asha, for being there

Acknowledgements

For all the teachers, staff and students in Zespol Szkol Ekonomicznych in Minsk Mazowiecki, a warm and hearty thanks for your hospitality, friendship and humour. I will never forget you. I'd like to extend a special thanks to Stefan Stepniewski, Anna Zimnicka, Malgorzata Grusaczynska and Anna Frelak.

To the APSO group of 1994, it was great to have known you and hope you are all in good places. To the guys – John Joe, Keith, Gearoid and Paul, stay in touch. And to Barry, a late arrival, your help and support with this book was invaluable, sorry you think the title sucks. And to Eamonn Crowley and Padraig Coll for their generosity.

To Rafal and Peter in Radio Polonia for their experience and support and to Magda Sowinska and Nath Espino, formerly of the *Warsaw Voice*. Without all of their help, none of what I am doing now would have been possible.

To those who have departed – Asha's father, Jurek, I wish there had been more time. To Fr Andrzej Pyka, a great friend to the Poles in Ireland who will be dearly missed. And Ollie Morgan, a man who helped so many in so many ways, we'll miss you.

Finally, to all at O'Brien Press for putting their faith in this book, especially Eoin, Michael and Claire.

Contents

A Horse with no Name

Summer 1994. It is late afternoon, the heat lingering from another day of intense sunshine. I never imagined this country could get so hot. But here it is, a brutal, dry heat that stings like an iron and makes everything appear rigid. Clothes hang outside on balconies around the town, stiff as playing cards. Windows gape open, gasping for breath. The playground is a patchwork of dried grass and bald spots, with a swing buckling under the heat.

People move slowly, some on old black bicycles, some on foot, barely kicking up dust on streets of tarmac and old rock. It needs rain. It needs some colour. It even needs some noise.

We pull in through the gates of the school, just myself, a driver and a guide. It is kept well enough, but looks as if it needs a couple of grand for a face-lift. Weeds poke up between cracks in uneven concrete. Window panes look like chapped lips. Even the national flag droops limply from a pole inside the gate, weary and just about retaining its colours.

Standing inside the front door of the school is a small, balding man in his sixties, a cigarette between old fingers and a wide smile like a spade on his face. He shakes hands warmly and brings us inside to his office. He makes coffee in glasses, each glass heaped with two spoonfuls of tar-like granules that should really have passed through a percolator.

The room is in stark contrast to the streets of the town we have wound through. It is bright and spotless, and smells pleasantly of the greenery that invades from every corner. He motions to the seats around a large, well polished table, offering us cigarettes that have no filters. I decline, being on the verge of giving up. Anyway, I am thinking more of my empty stomach, and eye instead the bowl of fruit ripening in the window next to all the plants.

The coffee is strong and has no milk, and as it cools, large, hard flakes begin floating to the top like pieces of loose bark. I battle with the burning glass as the man, who I now realise is the school director, discusses the terms of my contract between nods of the head, smiles and count-less filterless cigarettes. He is the type of man that immediately puts a stranger at ease – smiles, a gentle voice, friendly gestures with the hands.

He bellows smoke as he speaks. It comes out of his mouth, and out of his nose. I think at one stage it will start to come out of his ears. If I am trying to quit smoking, I've come to the wrong place.

I was going to miss the rest of the group, each and every one of them. We were a mixed bunch, of all ages and with different levels of experience. Some were just out of college, some older, and all of us had very different reasons for being there. For two weeks we had been together at a converted monastery in Lublin, in the southeast of the country, drinking mostly, and making vague attempts at learning smatterings of Polish. Almost every night was spent bunking off to an exclusive club in the nearby city, and every morning we were at our desks in a local school by eight, cracking open bottles of fizzy mineral water, trying to get our tongues around the Polish language and melting in the heat.

The language was a tough one. I knew right then that I was never really going to master it. I got a lot of it into my head, but it rarely got as far as my mouth without a lot of thinking getting in the way. That disturbed me a little, as I had come here to teach a language myself. Some of the group coped better. You could spot them during the lessons – even with the hangovers they had a confidence about themselves, and bit into those foreign words like food they had already tasted. These were the ones who were going to make good teachers. I would have to work at it that bit harder.

There was no competition between anyone though. If anything, we all acted as crutches for each other. Some people were homesick; some were just sick. Some were nervous about teaching and others were nervous about the towns they were going to.

Then the time came for us to split up and go our various ways. A guy called John Joe from Mayo was first, and

this seemed fitting, as he had unofficially become something of a group leader, particularly for some of the girls.
He was sent to a place not far away called Swidnik, just
outside Lublin. In fact, a few days later he was back for a
visit, and to give us a rundown on his new home. It was
like bloody Ballymun, he said, with blocks as far as the
eye could see. He was in one of the blocks, sharing with a
bachelor or a divorcee, he hadn't figured out which yet. I
would have dreaded sharing with a stranger, but John Joe
relished the company.

Our numbers dwindled daily, and the bonds between
us were broken. We grew sad, then bored, and finally just
waited our turn. Sitting on a wall in the courtyard of the
monastery in the baking sun, the guys bare-chested, the
women sweating, we sipped on beers and watched our
new pals disappear one by one, like cattle. We wondered
where the hell they were being taken and how we would
all get to meet up again. All we were left with was a list of
addresses that nobody could read and mystifying phone
numbers composed of four digits and regional codes.

Then it was my turn, along with a group of others. We
visited several schools that day, dropping off colleagues
one by one until I was the last one left in the van. I had a
bad taste in my mouth. All the places we'd seen were
fairly grim – lonely outposts, barely mapped, that had the
driver going around in circles as the day wore on. They
were mostly villages with one main street, dying as it
reached the outskirts, to be swallowed up by flat, endless

countryside, fading into the horizon with barely a cow to provide a focal point.

Few of these villages seemed ready to cope with the arrival of a stranger. Bus stops and train stations, even petrol stations, were in the minority. A quick search for bars, general stores and supermarkets was fruitless. These villages seemed lost in time. Motionless and still, they hung there on the cusp of the modern world, some of their inhabitants just about hanging in there with them. But they held a beauty of their own.

Some of the living quarters were also stuck in that weird, grey area between the old and the new. One school had somehow forgotten they were getting a foreign teacher, a girl who smiled bravely as she was led up a flight of bare concrete steps and into a single room by the cleaning lady who had been forced to shoulder the blame. There were no curtains, a couch full of holes for a bed and a bathroom with a toilet the colour of a rotten lung.

The woman ranted and apologised profusely, waving frantically at everything as if with one swish of a magic wand she was going to transform the room into a boudoir fit for a sleeping beauty. Our unfortunate colleague smiled and thanked her. She was tough – she had already told us a lot of stories about a year spent in Bosnia during the war. A shoddy bathroom wasn't going to kill her.

We felt bad leaving her there alone though, and there was a short burst of hysterical laughter when we returned to the van. Back on the main road, there was barely a sign anywhere to say the place even existed, and I never passed near it again. Now, I can't even recall its name. But I'll never forget how it looked.

The tiny village of Sadowne was next. A place not really worth describing, its only significance is its proximity to the former death camp of Treblinka. This was the last stop for Paul, a guy roughly the same age and equally as bewildered as myself. He hesitated before stepping down from the van and onto the courtyard. There stood the school director, a rather solemn-looking man, gasping heavily on a cigarette and beckoning all of us inside to his office. There was no coffee on offer there, just a few abrupt words from the director. His expression tired, he didn't volunteer any false hopes that Paul would be having a year to remember. He simply recited Paul's duties as though reading from a shopping list.

From the office we were led to the living quarters, a single room next to a single Russian woman with a single kid. Immediately looking for an escape route, Paul asked the whereabouts of a bus or train station. The director gestured in the direction of the nearby woods and informed Paul that the train station was some distance away and that he could get a lift with him whenever he wanted. Paul looked at the woods, where a desiccated mud trail led between spindly grey trees before disappearing in a series of twists and bends. Where does the train go? To Warsaw. How far is that? About sixty kilometres.

Since I couldn't yet pronounce the name of the place I was headed for, I didn't ask if there was a transport link. I simply shook Paul's hand and left him there, stroking his chin pensively. Then we were back on the road.

The guide now turns to me and goes through the details in English, looking reassuringly pleased. I have Fridays free, if I want, and otherwise work about six teaching hours per day. Although there are a few guys in some of the classes, the school is mostly for girls between the ages of sixteen and early twenties, and there are two other English teachers here that I can work with. I am to focus on improving conversation skills and vocabulary, to generally introduce a more colloquial language into the class than the 'book' English the students are used to. After that, it is up to me. I try to look content, because my director does. So I nod firmly and shake hands with him.

I stand at the window of my new home and watch the van drive out through the gate, severing that last link I had with the group. It is starting to get dark now and a lump rises in my throat. My quarters are clean and spacious, but understandably bare. Just me, the hum of the fridge, an old radio the size of a breeze block that the director has left and the fading summer evening sky outside, bloody orange, black at the edges.

I had met a Polish guy in Dublin before I left, who told me that summer evenings are always colourful in Poland. He was right. Deep, warm colours hang before me, over a landscape as flat as a football pitch. The sun looks like a massive, slow-moving balloon, being carried off gradually into the west. At that hour of evening in summer in Poland the temperature is neither too hot nor too cold. It is a comforting warmth that calms the body and soothes the mind. I think after that long day, some of the rough places we have seen and the pang of loneliness that suddenly hits me, if it had been belting down with rain, I would just have turned around and gone home.

Unpacking for a year is an odd feeling. As you pull items out one by one, there is a sense of finality about it. It's not just a wash bag and a few books. There are things that suggest permanency, that remind you of home. Clothes that smell of home cooking. Towels with the scent of the washing powder your mother uses. Books and magazines with coffee rings on the covers. You stare at them and realise that, like you, they have travelled thousands of miles and won't see home again for twelve months. These simple objects take on a value that they never previously had.

I have three large bags with me, one of them a lot heavier than it was the night I packed it. I open the zip of this one first and began wrenching out the winter clothes that lie at the top – heavy socks, gloves, a scarf and some 'long johns', that were eventually used to polish my boots. Below the clothes I had packed a few books and there, in the middle, lies the cause of the bag's weight – a statue of Our Lady and a heavy, wooden photo frame. Pictures of my family and friends smile up at me from under a clean piece of glass. Obviously, Ma got to the bag the night before I left, when my luggage was sitting downstairs by the door. Mothers mean well when they do such things. Religious relics are always a favourite, and so are family photographs, but I don't need to see all that right now.

The statue goes onto the window-ledge in the hall. The photos drive me to bed, feeling like a stranger should feel in a strange land – lonely, isolated and exhilarated, but strangely anonymous. I know nobody and nobody knows me. If I dwell long enough on that fact I will lapse into a state of panic as my mind balloons to encompass the whole of this country – 312,685 square kilometres, and thirty-six million people contained in it. And then me, a tiny, insignificant speck.

Lying there in bed with the room still basking in warmth, I begin to go over the images I had conjured up for myself before arriving, comparing them with what I have seen so far. You don't expect a thousand volts of culture shock coming to a place like this. It's not the centre of Africa or the Middle East. It's still Europe, but it's a part of Europe that most of us have only peeped at while it was hidden behind the iron curtain. So question marks hang over almost every aspect of life here.

I had been told many things, a lot of them tinged with a type of black humour that didn't always help. One girl who had spent a year in Warsaw offered me a piece of information by way of reassurance about a month before I left. 'You can get cornflakes there,' she had said, her smile fading rather miserably once she realised that cornflakes weren't high on my list of priorities. I had pictured instead the bowl they were in – a deep, wooden bowl paired off with a spoon cut from cheap tin that made a harsh sound when dropped on a stark kitchen floor. In that bowl I saw a lot of soups, made from thick vegetables and stringy meat, meat that came from an animal that had worked hard all its life. A horse maybe, with a shaggy coat, a massive pair of blinkers and no name, the remainder of his carcass finishing up as glue on the bench of a peasant carpenter.

I had pictured timber houses, smoke gasping out of their chimneys day and night, sitting under the shadow of grey blocks that clawed the landscape like broken umbrellas. I had pictured old men with shattered teeth, young girls with bright blonde hair, packed under scarves decorated with the flowers of spring. Fields that were golden in autumn and steel blue in winter. Cold vodka, warm beds and the sound of men singing in taverns, keeping a beat with the thud of beer tankards on long wooden tables. As I drift off to sleep, I think it is fair to say I have a rather confused image of Poland.

The Town that Lonely Planet Forgot

Hunger has a very discernible presence, despite its being derived from an absence. It is the first thing I notice the next morning, even before the shock of awakening in an alien environment.

It had been a long drive down the day before and there were no stop-offs. The school director had left some cold meat in the fridge, but I had eaten it all, straight from the packets with my fingers. There was also a bowl of fruit sitting on the table in my kitchen, but most of its contents had been given to the guide, who was also famished. The rest was tarnished by the fruit flies that had managed to rally themselves into a strong and determined congregation overnight. I eventually zapped them with a deodorant can and a box of matches as they flew around the centre of the room in a perfect circle.

At least it's sunny again. I can see the buttery yellow glow on the brown linoleum floor. If a pin dropped on that floor it would sound like lumber crashing on the floor of a forest. The place is as quiet and peaceful as a tomb. There is also a smell in the flat – not altogether unpleasant, just a strange smell, a bit like vinegar. Maybe they used it to clean the windows before I arrived – vinegar with sheets of newspaper, just like my grandmother had done. All homes have their own smells and this one is mine now for the next twelve months. I wish I had taken along something with a pungent scent of home.

I venture into my bathroom, which has no floor. That is, no recognisable floor. A cold, grey platform of rough screed, it is decorated with a bath propped up by four stumpy legs and a large poor-mouth bowl for a neighbour. I don't like these bowls. They look distressed, as if they're constantly yawning at you. They also have a shelf that catches everything and leaves it there in the open until you flush. Why, I could never understand.

The walls of the bathroom, as with the rest of the flat, are painted a safe and warm cream colour. In the top corner, over the bathtub, a cast-iron grate with a pattern like a torn stocking offers the only form of ventilation. And from the ceiling, a solitary bulb, butt naked, hangs like a dead man from a length of wire. I make a mental note to get a shade for that light, but never get around to it. I also make a mental note to get more colour into the place – a few posters maybe, paintings, something. If it weren't for the greenery outside and the flashes of red on the communist-style signs around doorways, the eye would have little colour to distract it.

The hot water is off, because school hasn't started yet, so I lean into the tub and splash a handful of cold water on my face and chest before gazing into the mirror. One of the greatest afflictions of western man is the fact that he spends most of the day living inside his own head. It's not a good thing. If you could have been inside mine at this time you would have seen demons. I have lost weight already, which I can't afford to do. My rib cage is like a washboard, my cheeks like inverted coconut shells. After roughly a quarter-century on the planet, I have only accumulated about ten stone, and I imagine a lot of it is going to be lost in this place. I need to get some food.

I get dressed in clothes that stick in the heat and go out into the main corridor. There are about ten doors on either side, including one into a washroom, and another self-contained flat just like mine at the far end. I wonder who lives there, because someone plainly does. There is a frosted glass window with a large plant just visible inside.

I stroll down the corridor, my footsteps sounding like the clatter of a ball in a squash court. This is just one wing of a very large building that will soon be home to hundreds of students. By the looks of the names on the doors – 'Jarek', 'Marek', 'Piotr' and so on – this section is for boys only, which is disappointing, but safe.

On my way out the front door I meet one of the women who showed me round my flat yesterday evening. She must work in the school as a cleaner or cook, or maybe both. She is bubbly and friendly and, having no English, went to great lengths demonstrating how my bed worked – a contraption that isn't really a bed at all, but a couch that springs into a bed after a series of short, snappy manoeuvres. They use them here instead of beds since beds take up space. She introduces me to her daughter, a gorgeous- looking girl with eyes like a pair of hazelnuts. She smiles, nods politely and extends a hand quickly. She doesn't speak much English, but her friend, a young guy of maybe seventeen, speaks English pretty well. At least he's confident, and offers to show me round the town. I ask him about a supermarket and he looks mildly confused, asking me exactly what it is I want. When I tell him I just need a general store he scratches his head before finally setting off, lost somewhat in thought.

The three of us skip down a side road that is collapsing in sand, hopping over grey and red bricks that sit in tidy little piles. Uneven, patchy and sinking at every second step, it looks like Beirut. They are building new footpaths, my companion tells me. And new apartments, and new roads, and a lot of other new things that are needed for a better infrastructure. Next I am told that that not many people will speak English. He tells me not to bother learning Polish. It is too difficult, and even a bold attempt will be a waste of time. He tells me that it is not always sunny here, and not to expect good weather once the summer ends. He also tells me that there is little or nothing to do. He tells me that I will be bored. In fact, he does his best to convince me that I have made a big mistake.

We stop outside a large shop with a charming wooden front and the word 'Delicatessy' painted across the top in red, giving it a Hansel-and-Gretel appearance. He insists that I can get everything I want inside, while he waits outside.

The shop is unusually wide but only about six feet deep, since the area for the public is abruptly cut off by an enormous length of counter. Behind this, all the produce is lined up in regimental style on shelves, the customers in front in a stiff and slow-moving queue. Most of them are old, the women in plain dresses, gripping string bags, the men in ill-matching trousers and jackets gripping the edge of the counter. They breathe heavily and wait patiently.

Those at the front of the queue slowly call out items, hesitating and searching the shelves with the tips of their fingers in the hope of finding what they came here for. Once the object is found on the shelf, the assistant, dressed in red apron, turns and stares at it for a moment as if to affirm its existence before moving toward it at the pace of a slug. The item is placed on the counter and the next one called out.

Apart from the voices of the assistants and the customer at the top of the queue, there is little noise. People just gaze and wait, as if the day ahead has little else for them. Some turn to look at me, but it isn't a look of hostility, it is simply a look. The objects on the shelves are unrecognisable. Even the pictures on the tins make no sense. Chopped meat of some sort. Cucumber perishing in a large jar of pickle.

'Didn't get anything?' my new friend asks when I come out.

'No. Maybe you can show me to a butcher's?'

This is no better. The shop is like a small wooden hut and there is a large woman with a knife cutting a great slab of meat between her breasts, surrounded by every insect with a pair of wings.

'Maybe you fancy a pizza?'

He takes me to the train station about half a mile from my home. The grey and rather drab-looking building sits like crude Lego, the words 'PKP Minsk Mazowiecki' in harsh chunky letters across the flat roof. The lettering is redolent of communism, its form direct, imposing and menacing. Even the shape of the station building breaks all laws of aesthetics. It looks like it was just dropped there from the end of a crane.

Directly in front of the station, taxis snooze in the sun, the drivers' heads gazing up momentarily with each squeak of the station doors. The line is long, the engines cold. The drivers all wear similar shirts of browns, blues and greys, all with their sleeves rolled up. The cars vary. There is the odd Mercedes, shining like a new coin in between cars that I have never seen before. Tiny little battered things like matchboxes wrapped in tinfoil that I later learn are called 'maluchs', which actually means 'tinies'. Few people seem eager to rush to the taxis, so most of the drivers are asleep.

To the left, a small, wooded park hides the bus depot, where groups of kids sit on benches under trees, chomping on hotdogs from nearby kiosks. Like the taxis, the buses don't seem to be going anywhere. They look old and clapped out, single-deckers with their destinations displayed on cards shoved onto their dashboards.

I am led to the pizza restaurant, but as we sit, I realise it isn't really a restaurant at all – more of a snack bar, sitting at the end of a long line of similar snack bars, none of which is very inviting. The pizzas are fished out of a freezer, cooked in a microwave, then presented on a plate as if freshly baked. The bottom is soggy, the ingredients strange. Peas, carrots and pickle. But at least it is cooked food.

I buy my two companions Cokes and as I eat I am asked a lot of questions, the answers not coming very freely. I have only been here a day and already I have discovered that curiosity knows no bounds. The same sense of bewilderment stretches from the young to the old; nobody can understand why the hell a 'rich man from the west' – as they put it – would want to come to a small town so randomly located in the east of Poland at such a time.

And it is randomly located. If you can cast your mind back to geography class and the reasons why an area is first settled, you'd be hard pressed to recall one that could explain the existence of Minsk Mazowiecki. It is nowhere near the coast. From what I can see, there are no longer any mineral deposits or any natural resources of any kind. On the map of the region it looks like a mistake. On the map of the country it is barely a black dot. In fact, it has a history as a settlement that goes back to the fifteenth century and began its life on the banks of the Srebrna (silver) River. The Srebrna has long since lost both its shimmer and its status as a river, and is now more of a brackish stream. Minsk is really just a satellite town, one of many that have developed along the rail track from Warsaw to Russia.

Little of any historical note seems to stand out. In fact, there is little that stands out at all. The town has a park where grass does its best to grow. In the centre of the park lies the standard cultural centre that all Polish towns have. They are generally called 'the Palace' and are used for concerts and meetings. This one also has a restaurant in its basement. There is a church, a few schools, the obligatory army barracks and one or two shopping streets. The stores vary in style from modern brick buildings to old wooden ones that just about hang in there, but at least give some sense of a past. After that, there are a few sprawling residential quarters, again made up of modern blocks and wooden homes.

That is about it. It isn't exactly ugly, just lacking something, and like a lot of towns near Warsaw really serves a basic function – in this case, giving people somewhere to live. But the most alarming fact of all is that there is no entry for the town in my Lonely Planet guide.

These guides are honest. If a place is good it says it's good. If a place is a dump then it says so. And destinations both good and bad can contribute to the travel experience. But if a place isn't mentioned at all then only one conclusion can be drawn – there is, quite frankly, no reason for going there.

As for the timing? Well, I am here precisely because times are hard. Communism is not long toppled and the place is a bit of a mess. Their government asks our government for help. So they get me, and the eighteen others who are right now wandering around similar towns and villages, being asked the same questions.

So, to answer all their questions, I lie. A little. I lie a little because I haven't figured it all out myself yet. I haven't had time to think about it. From the application to the interview process was only a matter of weeks. The training flew by and before we knew it we were packing our bags. But I have a feeling that time is something I am going to have plenty of here.

I tell them I want to teach in Poland because I have met some Polish people before and I became very fond of them. I tell them I am tired of hearing about people going to other countries to work. I tell them that I think Poland is an interesting country to visit and that I might learn something from the experience.

They're not convinced. The young girl throws a vacant stare back at me and fiddles with her straw. The guy just shakes his head and sighs. Both responses amount to the same thing – they just can't understand what I am doing here.

It had never occurred to me that these people would be gob-smacked at the thought of someone leaving the West to work in the East when thousands are trying to do exactly the opposite. It is as if they find the whole thing cynical or insulting in some way, that there is a certain luxury available to me that I can do such a thing at this stage of my life. It is an aspect of voluntary work that I had never considered. Many people resent charity, and the Polish people are a proud, resilient nation. I will have to think of a better reason for being here, I decide, something that will sound more convincing at least. I made the decision to give a period of my life to help those less fortunate. I want to do some good. And I do genuinely want to devote a couple of years to teaching. The two will work together, I thought. But I will have to do better than that if I am going to convince the Poles. Besides, calling the Polish people 'less fortunate' would be a great mistake.

We walk idly round the town for the rest of the afternoon, picking out landmarks and placing them mentally in distances from my home. The young kid, whose name is Jarek, drops the odd interesting remark about the town he lives in, but there is a jaded tone in everything he says. The girl, Agnieszka, smiles mostly and says very little. And I wonder how they fill their days here. What do they do on a long summer holiday in the town? What do they look forward to?

They lead me to another supermarket down on the main road, the road that runs all the way to Russia and rumbles occasionally from the weight of large trucks with foreign stickers on the back. This supermarket, thankfully, is self-service, but it isn't well stocked. It is also full of half-dressed firemen from the depot across the way, bored with the heat, buying single bottles of beer and flirting with the giggling assistants. Single bottles of beer are a common feature in Poland, where a customer can stroll into a shop and purchase a bottle from the fridge, drink it at the counter, then leave.

When I enter, the giggling ceases and the assistants stare, one following my every move round the shop with her eyes. When I go down towards the back, she leaves her counter quietly and efficiently, as if on wheels, and stands directly behind me, arms folded. In a bit of a panic I grab some cheese, ham, bread, what I presume is soup and as many bottles of beer as I can fit into a bag.

The clatter of these bottles raises the eyebrows of my two new friends when I come out. I thank them, telling them I can find my own way back. They smile politely and I shake hands and walk the other way, the clinkety-clink of the beer bottles one of the only sounds on the quiet streets.

When I get home it is around five o'clock and the main room basks in a deep orange. I load up the fridge with the few bits of food and the myriad bottles and wonder how I can kill the evening off quickly and efficiently. It needs to be murdered because it is going to be a long one.

As the fridge fills up and the light at the back dims, I start to feel a bit guilty. I never fancied the thought of drinking alone before, and so never did. Who do you talk to? How many can you take and when do you stop? And what about the following night when you're sitting here again with nothing to do? I finally decide not to care. It is going to be a long, lonely night and sleep will not come easily.

So that evening, at the end of my first real day here, I sat down with the windows open and began writing letters to as many friends as I could, each one concluded with a bottle of strong Polish beer, the envelope sealed with stringy spit. Lord knows what I wrote. Writing a long letter is a poor substitute for conversation.

With letters done and the sun setting, I found company in a new acoustic guitar that I had taken with me and which cost what I would probably earn here in a year. I had been playing for years, but I would get to play that guitar so much in Poland that the frets would eventually become like flattened matchsticks.

I wondered what the other Irish guys were up to, whether they had gone down the same route as myself and had stocked up on alcohol to make the opening of this chapter in our lives that bit gentler. For emigration means opening a new chapter. You remove yourself from the norm and anything is possible. Who knew how things would go? You could fall in love with the place and remain for the rest of your days. You could swing the other way and return home after a matter of weeks. Or you could do your time, enjoy it, take the rough with the smooth, work hard and meet as many people as possible. People who, in years to come, when all was in the past, would be nothing more than distant but charming memories, their fates and whereabouts unknown. Some would have been closer to you than others, but all would have contributed in some way to the colourful experience that you would never had known had you stayed in the one place. It was all there ahead of us.

With darkness settled outside, I sat on the couch and went through some of the cassettes I'd put together, not being able to take my CD collection along. Tom Waits became a favourite, with one album in particular, 'Nighthawks at the Diner', getting a lot of airing at night with the beers. There were so many stories there, set in the groove of a light jazzy accompaniment that was just so soothing and homely. One track on that album is 'Better Off Without a Wife', which I used to quote liberally from without any idea of what Poland had in store for me.

As the music played and a warm breeze floated through the open windows, kicking the curtains up like skirts, I felt good. The light in the fridge grew brighter as it was emptied of bottles and I decided, in my high spirits, that I would work out some good reasons for being there, a reason why I was doing my utmost to get away from a career path at home to come to a small town in Poland to teach in a State school. I thought long and hard, and came up empty-handed. So I gave up thinking.

I didn't need a reason. I wanted to get away, and could have ended up anywhere. Something took me to this place and that was that. I started to believe in a destiny of sorts, that it was impossible for people to plan on ending up in situations like this and that it wasn't merely down to a roll of the dice. If chance couldn't be that random with people's lives and plans like this aren't really made, then there must be something or someone else at the controls that had it all worked out for us. I liked that idea, so I went with it. But it still wouldn't convince the Poles.

Lady in a Glass Case

Day two was a Sunday and I was woken early by bells. It must have been just after dawn. They went on for what seemed a long, long time.

I fell back asleep and the next time I woke it was the rain I was hearing. It came down like something out of the Old Testament, pounding the windows like buckshot, and now I had a blinding headache. Instead of the buttery sun spread out on the lino, a large pool of water crawled from the ground beneath the window before snaking out towards the rug in the centre of the floor. I stood and waded through it barefoot, lifting the soggy curtains slowly from the sill. The windows looked frail, the paint peeling, the wood beneath starting to crumble like a sodden cigarette. If the rain gets in, what's going to stop the cold when winter falls? Abandoning that thought, I jammed a couple of towels under the frames and got dressed to go foraging for food once more.

Outside, puddles turned to ponds and the sandy pavements became scarred with rivulets, threatening to pull the ground from beneath like a rug. The supermarket on the main road that had yesterday saved my life was closed, so I walked further, halting at a roadside statue of

Our Lady in a glass case. I stood under a tree to shelter from the rain, still coming down in buckets. The statue reminded me of the one that now sat in my hallway and I wondered briefly if I was being followed. If I was, then I prayed I would be guided towards food and some solace, because I needed it that morning.

From an old church down the road, a large, white building with steeples that more resembled the churches of Russian Orthodoxy than Roman Catholicism, people filed out with black umbrellas and walked bent over into a sheet of rain. Some of them stopped and entered a small building on the far side of the road, near the park. It was a rather plain building, square, with net curtains and simple tables visible inside. One of the old communist-style bars that served beer, coffee and food measured out in grams – sausage, bread and butter. I wasn't brave enough to go in. So, bidding adieu to Our Lady in the glass case, I pulled my jacket up around my ears and set off.

I chanced upon a small, wooden grocery store worked by an old but strong-looking man, a clean, white coat tied at his waist. We soon devised a system of communication. I point at something and he points with me and when I nod he makes sure of the choice by holding whatever it is in the air and raising his eyebrows. I nod again and he lays it on the counter, scribbling down the price for a tot on a sheet of brown paper that eventually goes to wrap up a lump of ham. I also managed to get bread, thank the Lord, a few bananas, eggs and a packet of imitation Jaffa

Cakes, the luxury item in the day's catch. Apart from the imitation Jaffa Cakes, it occurred to me that finding convenient food here was going to be difficult.

That particular Sunday was one of the worst days I spent in Poland. From the church bells at dawn to the buckets of rain, and the feelings of envy watching families and elderly people file into that old communist-style 'stolowka' for lunch. I missed home dinners and I missed home. With only myself for company, I was bored beyond belief and keen just to start working.

The days were long after that. Jarek called again a few days later but I turned down the offer of help or another tour, for some reason preferring the solitude of the vacant flat. Anyway, I was quite happy arranging everything in the flat to suit myself. There was a surprising amount of space, with a large living room/bedroom (depending on whether you'd converted the couch or not), a hall, a bathroom, a kitchen and a spare room that was eventually just used as a dumping ground for books and drunken visitors.

On the whole, I'd done rather well. The flat was really too much for one person, and I had been told by the guide that it was originally home to a whole family. It was clean, if basic, and clearly a lot of effort had been made for me. I took this as a good sign. It meant that the people here cared. They cared about me before they'd even met me, which must be a good indication of their hospitality.

The view out of the main window was hardly inspiring, but it was genuinely pleasant – a large block on the left, the ground floor of which housed a kindergarten, and the main school buildings visible on the right beyond a small green where children from the kindergarten played. There was a laneway that had yet to be paved and tarmacked on the left also, all mud and puddles. Where it led I didn't know at this stage. In the distance a variety of wooden houses, brick houses and other nondescript buildings stretched out towards the train line, beyond that only fields.

I kept the windows open all the time. Apart from the rain on the Sunday, it was hot during the day, and in the evenings the heat would be replaced by a pleasant air carrying with it a scent of warm moisture and coal smoke. I would stand at the window and watch the sky dim and the fields become obscured. The houses would gradually disappear until, finally, there would be nothing but darkness. I liked those evenings. I would drink one beer after the next, watching this transformation from day to night. By the time it got dark I was almost fit for bed. And I would wonder where all the people were in this town. It seemed to just grind to a standstill once night fell.

In the mornings I would wake and take a minute to remind myself where I was. Then I would take a look around the flat, maybe fix up one more room, unpack a bit more, and plan what to do with the place for the year.

Still lacking the courage to queue in the main store for proper food, I was driven to the pizza restaurant a number of times over the next few days, until some old woman farted at me. I can still picture her perfectly. She stood outside a planked-up wooden house, sucking the guts out of a cigarette, idly examining the evening. Short legs planted into a pair of furry slippers, she fixed me with a stare from some way off. Then as I passed, she winced up one eye and farted loudly. Maybe she didn't mean it. But I won't forget that fart. It was the only form of human communication in days.

Class Acts and Strange Tongues

In contrast to the quiet of the previous few days, the day school started was mayhem. The night before it was due to commence, the students began arriving in droves to take up their rooms on corridors that had until then been like a tomb. It had been explained to us that all schools have their boarding blocks, but that didn't mean they were all boarding schools. Kids would come from remote villages or towns scattered across the province or even further, and rather than face long journeys on infrequent buses through cold winters, would instead stay in the blocks for a very small fee, since the schools were essentially run by the State.

I sat up for hours that night, distracted by the chaos of slamming doors, screaming kids who hadn't seen each other all summer and a discordant mix from a variety of stereos playing a variety of music.

Poring over the books and notes that I'd taken with me, I realised I hadn't a clue how I was going to get through it. Too many years in college had put the idea in my head that I wanted to teach. It was the necessary extension of a long period of academia without any practical applications. In fact, it was the only route I wanted to go down, because I was really a domesticated college animal. Business, uniforms, suits and nine-to-five jobs held no interest for me whatsoever.

But as I sat there that night reading over the notes from the training school, I realised that I'd no idea where to even begin. Teaching is a vocation and, like many vocations, it can call on those who have the heart, but perhaps not the expertise, to deliver. It occurred to me that evening that maybe I was one of those poor souls. Good intentions are not always good enough.

The instructors in the school in Dublin had bent over backwards to prepare us. We had spent weeks in mock lessons, experimenting on Spanish and Italian kids who had volunteered to be taught by the teachers who had never taught before. Throughout the training a lot of worrying issues were raised regarding the schools to which we were being sent. Tape recorders, televisions, photocopiers, proper books and possibly even chalk would be lacking, so we were warned to prepare and to take with us any amount of props that could be used to get us out of sticky situations – regular and irregular verbs written on stiff pieces of cardboard and laminated; articles from magazines; photographs, books and lots of coloured markers. But I was still trying to come to grips with the complexities of English grammar. The ability to speak and write your native language doesn't qualify you to explain its make-up. The more I thought about it, the more I realised that there were an infinite number of questions that could leave me stumped up there.

Also bothering me was the fact that the Polish language differs so greatly from ours and is, in fact, missing what we would take to be basic elements in language. There are no articles, for example. If the Poles are used to saying, 'Cat walks down street,' how can you convince them to put 'a' or 'the' in front of the nouns? Worse still, how do you explain when it's 'a' and not 'the'? The Polish language also lacks the perfect tenses. 'He has been here twice this morning,' doesn't make any sense. 'He was here twice this morning,' is adequate in Polish. Also, because of the amount of cases their language contains, there is no need for a definitive word order in sentences. Where we must put, for example, place, frequency and time in the correct order, for the Poles it makes no difference. 'Twice to the cinema went I last week,' is a well-constructed sentence in Polish.

I was staring at time charts that showed you how to carefully divide up a forty-five-minute period so the students don't lose sight of your goal. Then there were the problems of the goal itself, which should be based on a language function, a concept to present that language function, a medium through which to present that concept and a method of checking to see if it was fully understood at the end. I don't remember any of that from when I was in school. Maybe that was because the teachers all spoke the same language as me. Now, somehow, we were supposed to teach English, through English, to people who had no English. The trainers in Dublin had a convincing enough logic for doing this, but eleven thousand miles away in a remote town in Eastern Europe, the same logic just didn't seem very compelling at all.

When I finally got to bed I think I must have prayed myself to sleep. I prayed that I would be forgiven for thinking I was a teacher. I prayed that if I was going to try to be a teacher, that the Lord would come halfway and help me. I even reasoned with Him, offering up the view that I was really here to do a good service for people and, in a world with more evildoers than good, I deserved a break. He did come halfway, actually. But that's about as far as He got.

At half-past eight the next morning, after a night where sleep came only in fits and starts, two large pairs of knuckles battered the paint off my hall door. I knew there were two pairs because of the incredible racket and because of the hollow clatter of four high-heeled feet coming down the corridor beforehand. I was already beginning to detect some odd habits in the Polish people. Knocking on doors, for one, was extremely rare, and was not meant as a request, but a warning. Sure enough, no sooner had the knocking faded but the door handle was being wrenched out of its socket like a limb. So, this was my first introduction to the teachers. Thankfully, I had anticipated it and locked the door overnight.

The knuckles belonged to two women, English teachers, who had come too early – another distinctly Polish habit – to escort me to the opening ceremony. One was older and seemed on the brink of retirement, the other was younger and broke into a giggle when I opened the door in nothing but a pair of trousers. Both stared at me as I scurried between the bathroom and bedroom in a fluster, making myself look respectable for my first day.

Once outside we slammed into a wall of heat and I immediately began to sweat. My bowels rumbled with nerves. The shirt itched. The collar was hard and tight on my neck. The trousers were too heavy. But this was the opening ceremony and all ceremonies, big or small, are important events here. They involve the staples of music – preferably with a good parp of brass – plenty of speeches and applause, an abundance of flowers and immaculate dress.

In the main hall, several hundred students were assembled in rows of seats, with several hundred more standing at the back. The noise was like a local football derby, and only for a stunning Polish girl running up and presenting me with flowers at the door, I probably would have wet a portion of my new trousers. She planted a kiss on each cheek, which took me by surprise, and, after exchanging a few words of welcome, dashed away into the mob like a startled deer before I could even get her phone number.

I took a seat near the front, nodding keenly at random individuals along the way, doing my best to look as if I already belonged. But I could feel the eyes behind me, along with the giggles and whispers and the prods of fingers in mid-air.

It was natural for the girls to be staring, surely. Not only was I the sole foreigner on the staff, I was also the youngest and, by the looks of it so far, the only male. It was an enviable position to be in, if it weren't for the fact that this was a school and I had a responsible position in it. I focused on the prospect of having to get up in front of all these girls and make them learn the English language. That, and the appearance of another young male teacher, soon drove any other thoughts out of my head.

The ceremony began with what I gathered to be the National Anthem and a student body, consisting of four girls dressed in white blouses and short black skirts, marching in from the corridor with a flag. I couldn't keep my eyes off them, distracted only when I had to stand and bow as the director introduced me as the new English teacher. Finally, after various speeches and applauses, the student body stood again with the flag and the whole assembly filed out and into the classrooms.

Lessons actually began quite well. At least, I was able to remain reasonably composed. I had been practising a strut of confidence on my empty corridor, and the technique of not looking up until I was at the desk with the ledger open. I remembered teachers in school who did this, and they were all bastards. Not that I wanted to be a bastard, but there was just something authoritative about it, I felt. That technique didn't last too long. Ignoring the students at the beginning of each lesson is a bad way to start.

In the beginning, it was all trial and error of course. When you walk into a foreign class for the first time you don't know how good their English is. So you rant on anyway, until you realise they haven't a clue what you're saying. Staring back at you wide-eyed like budgies on a perch, their awful silence steadily creeps into a whisper before lurching forward into chaos. Before you know it, you've lost control of thirty-five teenage girls. And you won't get it back. It is the longest forty-five minutes you will ever have to live through. Because of a few pretty bad days early on, I learned a number of basic rules quite quickly.

You have to learn all their names. That means all of them. There is nothing as devastating for a teenager than to be the only one who appears to have been forgotten by the teacher. It is like having a bad skin disease or some horrendous smell disorder. So, I asked them all to write their names down on large pieces of paper and place them on their desks in the mornings.

The word got round the school quite quickly that this was my method, and immediately all the girls in the new classes had made large name tags from pieces of white card. By day two it had almost become a competition. Almost. Some were fastidiously coloured in, with flowers, the seaside or pictures of an eye winking with long lashes.

Others were simply scrawls. I could quite quickly separate the more diligent and creative students from the lay-abouts, simply by the amount of effort they put into these name cards, and was quite proud of my early forays into classroom psychology.

The first ten minutes of every lesson was taken up with me making an arse of myself trying to pronounce their names and admiring their handiwork. But I was quite prepared to make an arse of myself, if it meant they got a laugh and the ice was broken a bit. When I was finished doing that I'd throw in a story about me going round the town trying to get things done, adding a smattering of bad Polish for an extra chortle. That was obviously a gas for them – the Irish clown trying to buy his groceries.

Of course, this was a grave error. I forgot that most of these girls lived in the same town. From then on, whenever I went into a shop I'd be watched and studied like some rare species of animal that had moseyed in by mistake.

The curiosity of the students never ceased to amaze me. Some were immediately brazen and would stand and ask questions in fabulous English, which for a new teacher was very encouraging. A lot of them would simply stare at you, like the folk in the shop – not a stare of ill will at all, just a stare or a smile. Maybe they weren't used to many foreigners. Maybe I was odd. But so many of these stares would be possessed of looks of such fragility that I was struck hard by thoughts about their backgrounds, what some of them may have gone through, and the possibilities that lay ahead. I realised very quickly how placid the Poles were as a race – apart from some of the lunatics on the street I would eventually get to know – a placidity that was torn apart so many times throughout their history. So when I met a stare in the class, I felt taken with a sense of responsibility that was often uncomfortable.

Within a few days I had also started to figure out what kind of school I was in. When I arrived, the name of the school was just a jumble of letters over the main door – 'Zespol Szkol Economicznych'. Other schools could be called 'Technikum' or 'Zawadowa'. Although to all of us who arrived here they were simply schools, your sanity and career could depend on exactly where you were placed.

As opposed to the general education system at home, where you go to school, do the obligatory subjects and have a fairly limited choice for your leaving certificate, the Polish education system acknowledges the fact that not all students are academic. That may sound a little condescending, but it is a simple fact of life. Not everybody has the inclination or ability to get through English, maths, Irish, geography and history, with further hopes of attending a university. Some are academic; some are more technically minded; some are creative; others plan to live on a farm. The Polish school system, then, is broken down into many categories for the student – technical schools, mechanical schools, catering schools, professional schools, schools of economics, language and academic schools, farming schools and so on. Because APSO didn't want to be seen as elitist by sending everybody to serve in a language or economic school, some of us ended up in technical and mechanical schools.

The project was a bit of a disaster in that respect. It was never going to work, but it took some time to realise that. Some teachers had success stories, particularly a few of the girls who had been given jobs in primary schools. The kids in these schools loved them, and many teachers stayed well beyond their one-year contracts. A few handled the language schools very well and were well received. But there were schools that really didn't care less whether or not a new teacher had arrived, be it from the West or the East.

However, only one girl went home that first year. She had been sent to a town farther away in the remote east of Poland, a vast, bleak area that has little to console an expatriate. She was living in a classroom, with a curtain separating her bed. Every morning she would be woken by the kids peering in at her, with that odd, endlessly curious stare. So she packed her bags.

To be fair to the students, and without trying to disparage the teachers in any way, years of inferior methods and forced learning had crippled the Polish education system to a great degree. It all began with the Russians. From the moment of their occupation, they drove the Russian language down the throats of the Poles, starting with the letter 's'. Why 's'? The staple textbook, even for the kids in primary school, was *Stalin, Voprozy Leninizma* (*Stalin, Studies in Leninism*). While they were at it, they rewrote the history of modern Poland. The Katyn massacre, the deportations, the shootings, the gulags, the Warsaw Rising, were all conveniently left out.

Teaching methodology also laboured under the communist system, and with it any urge to be innovative. We were trained to teach creatively, to demonstrate and create rather than simply translate. If you needed to communicate the word 'chicken', you simply pranced around like a twit, flapping imaginary wings until you heard a communal 'Aaaah' and a collective nod of heads.

Ultimately you had no choice, since you couldn't speak their language, but this form of demonstration baffled some and amused others. For students unused to such methods it was going to prove difficult, and there would inevitably be those who would not adapt at all. However, it was bound to be better than the 'book' English that the director had referred to. If they managed to learn anything at all from these books, it's unlikely it would ever be understood by anyone in the English-speaking world.

The books the students were using at the time were hardback beasts that sat in glass cases at the back of the rooms, under lock and key. The teacher would come into the class, open the presses and dish out the books. With one black-and-white illustration per chapter, the first chapter was titled something like 'A Day at the Zoo'.

The illustration at the top of the page showed a few kids in uniform, together with a teacher in uniform, standing near a cage and staring at a zebra. It read, *Today, teacher took her class to the zoo. A zoo is a public institution where living animals are exhibited. In this cage there is a zebra, which is a strikingly patterned, black and white equine animal from the grasslands of Africa.* The more difficult words – just about all of them – would be underlined and a glossary was provided at the end of the chapter with the words in Polish. The zoo chapter, incidentally, was probably the most useful in the real world, since other chapters might include 'A Day at the Museum of Industry' or 'Summer on a Collective Farm'.

Little wonder then that the bulk of kids weren't particularly interested in learning English. I never bothered with books, and spent five years designing my own lessons with the help of assorted 'Tips for TEFL Teachers'-style books. Some bombed, others didn't. Either way, I was burnt out by the end of it.

'I'm doing no teaching this year and I'm going to do less no teaching next year,' one of my colleagues said, going into his second year in a 'mechanical school'. He was fed up with guys who had no other calling but to drive or repair trains for the rest of their lives after they had served their stint in the army. Many of the guys in such schools, particularly in the last year or two prior to leaving, would get very depressed about the army, which was rife with bullying. There was little you could do to console them.

It wasn't from want of trying. No matter what my colleague did, they just wouldn't respond. They didn't want to speak English and, since most of them would go back to their country towns and villages to work, they never saw the need to speak English. The performing monkey from the West could stick his classroom antics up his behind. In the end, he agreed to let most of them play cards at the back of the room while he left a book open on the desk and went through the motions for the few interested parties at the front. It was the only thing to do.

The school I was assigned to was an economic school, thankfully, and the majority of the kids were girls who knew the value of foreign languages. It was also mixed with an art faculty filled with good-natured and intelligent kids, but who tended to get bored and wander into tortured-artist mode now and again. There were a few 'Zawadowa' (professional) student groups, training to become clerks and civil servants, and some tough post-leaving certificate students called 'Pomaturalne' (meaning 'post maturity', since the leaving certificate exam is called the 'maturity' exam).

This last group were older – about nineteen or twenty – and wearier, containing several hard guys who were simply there to avoid the army. Almost all, male and female, shared the same lack of vision when it came to learning English. For the most part, these were the ones who didn't get to university, and returned to school for a post-leaving education as a second choice. It wasn't altogether a bad choice, but I got the impression that it was still a second choice. They were a generally depressed bunch in school, although good fun outside it, swaggering in late and disappearing from the room before the bell for the end of the lesson had even begun to echo. If some of the younger kids had a problem figuring out my methods, then to the older mob I was a complete enigma. They played cards, swore in Polish, darted in and out for cigarettes and at times didn't show up at all. When that happened, I would have to go to the assistant director, a tough but fair woman, shrug, and say 'nie ma'.

This 'nie ma', literally translated as 'no has', was a handy phrase that could be used in a variety of circumstances to express the negative in Poland. And expressing the negative became quite useful, I discovered. In this case, it meant that the students were simply not there.

She would shake her head, then respond likewise with a casual shrug and a rather indifferent 'nie ma'. And that was that. I came to learn quite quickly that when something went wrong here it wasn't questioned much. It has gone wrong. And that's about it. It made life easier, true, but it also made it very bewildering.

A Place called Home

I was settling into the flat, making do with my own company as best I could. It's probably not a great thing to lead such a solitary existence. You become selfish, developing habits that wouldn't be accommodated by other people and viewing everyone that comes to the door with the wariness of a crack dealer. Sometimes, I would even imagine there was a knock on the door, but there would be nobody there at all.

The corridor that only a few weeks ago had reminded me of The Shining, was now thronged with guys between the ages of fifteen and early twenties. It was full of noise, testosterone, forbidden cigarette smoke and the odd clink of a vodka bottle in the smaller hours. That clink would strike a note of envy in me, as did the occasional giggle of a girl from one of the lads' rooms. But with the corridors of the boarding block, rather grimly known as the 'internat', patrolled ruthlessly by teachers on night duty, the vodka and the girls were more the exception than the rule.

Once dawn broke, I would be awoken by the boarding-block wake-up call, a penetrating brute of a noise emanating from a strategically placed bell that had become hoarse but resolute with age. Immediately following the bell, the competition for the showers would begin. The stampede on the corridors would be followed by agonising screams from the antiquated water pipes. I don't know which was worse, the bell with the throat cancer or the rheumatic water pipes. Either way, sleep was impossible in that building beyond 6.30am.

Other disturbances on my corridor were of the general prison variety – the odd fight, mad Polish heavy metal music, universal cries of angst and even football, which was played using my hall door as a goal. They didn't dare use the door at the far end, since that belonged to the Russian teacher. I quickly learned that anything with a Russian tag on it, even a Pole who taught the language, struck the fear of God into the folk here.

Evenings would be spent listening to the drumming of feet on the linoleum floor, punctuated every now and again by a hollow thud on my hall door and a loud, victorious cheer. Whenever I opened the door to go out, the guys would freeze momentarily, utter a polite 'Dobry wieczor' (good evening), then continue hammering the door once I had gone down the stairs.

They were harmless lads really. And while the younger guys would greet me with an almost uncomfortable courtesy, the older guys in the 'pomaturalne' classes tended to view me more as a peer. So much so, that some evenings a couple of them would knock on the door with a bottle of vodka and I'd invite them in. I wasn't terribly sure whether drinking with the students was the ethical thing to do, but I didn't particularly care. I was bored, and so were they. The fact that we couldn't really communicate didn't matter. We would drink, open dictionaries, swap words and pass the night. I would show photos and they would do likewise, broad grins plastered across their faces. Later I became very friendly with some of the older students. It made things a bit awkward the next morning in class, when the girls would laugh at our hangovers. Eventually I cut out the visits to my room and went out instead, reasoning that being in a bar with students was less likely to be frowned upon than being in the room.

There was a group of guys in one of these classes who were in their last year, and I grew very friendly with them. Robert, Piotr, Grzegorz and Mariusz, and two girlfriends of theirs, Monika and Agnieszka. They took me out several times to a bar near where they lived – not a great place at all, but it really didn't matter. It had pool tables, it had beer, and it had a bunch of guys and girls who used to take me there and walk me the whole way back, as they assured me the town wasn't very safe. Everyone knew I went out to the pub with these students, and the vice director even encouraged it. Once they finished school, however, I lost touch very quickly. Poles have to make a very fast transition from school to being bread winners. Life just takes over and that is it. But the intensity of the friendships that Poles instil – shortlived or not – stays with you.

There was another guy that first year – a decent fella,

nineteen or twenty, who didn't seem like the most indus-
trious guy in the school, but he gave it a go in my lessons
and I admired him for it. Now and again the pair of us
would sneak out past the teacher on night duty to the
local café to guzzle a few beers and trade words. Usually it
would be arranged, but one night he came banging on my
door, already pretty drunk. He insisted on going out and I
got the impression that something was up.

We got to the local café – just a poorly lit room where
kids sipped on cokes and a few of the older set sipped on
beers – and he began sinking bottles at an alarming rate.
Eventually, he turned to me and explained that he had got
a girl pregnant. Then he collapsed in a heap on the table
in front of me. All I could do was buy him another beer
and give him a slap on the back every couple of minutes
to try and encourage him. By the end of the evening he
was a sorry mess. A couple of weeks later he was gone,
and I never saw him again.

He was one of only a few guys in the older classes that
were genuinely trying, and it seemed a real shame. It
occurred to me that such circumstances demanded a very
different response here. Education had to be subordinate
to getting some sort of work, getting married right away
and looking after the kid. It was really a luxury that he
couldn't afford. There would have been no question of
him not marrying the girl, of not doing 'the right thing'. I
just hoped he loved that girl. But, judging by the amount
of beer he drank that night, I doubt it.

Poland was a deeply Catholic country, with a strict code of morals, particularly among the older people. I had a girlfriend at home at the time, who was due to come over for a short holiday. I was putting off telling the school director though, after I was taken into the office of the boarding school director one afternoon, with the elder of the English teachers as translator, to discuss any ideas I had concerning 'visitors'. With the door closed behind me, I was sat at the apex of a triangle of seats and fixed with a gaze from the boarding school director, a decent and rather quiet woman in her sixties. She told me, in a low voice as if from the confessional, that I was not permitted to have women, especially women 'of bad character', in my room. There was a pause to allow the words to sink in, followed by the question, 'You do know what we mean by women of bad character, Tom, don't you?'

I tried to figure out whether they meant me getting lucky around the town or whether I was the type to go down to the main road, the one that ran from Russia, to pick up hookers. Either way, it put the bloody frighteners on me. I got on the phone pronto to my girlfriend, telling her she'd better arrive as a tomboy or a lesbian because there was no way she was going to be allowed stay in my room.

In the end, I told them that a 'friend' was visiting for a holiday. When I came home from work that afternoon, a spare bed had been left in the hall. I don't think anyone actually believed me, but I had covered myself and managed to salvage both of our reputations. Sadly, we couldn't salvage the relationship, which more or less ended as soon as we saw that cast-iron bed.

Besides coming and going, the only time I wandered around the boarding building was to avail of the meals, which I was entitled to as a guest teacher. It was a decent gesture, but I gave it up after a few weeks, primarily because I couldn't handle the food. I also tended to be under some scrutiny from the students whilst eating and began to feel a bit like an animal at feeding time. 'What's he trying to do with that chop?' I imagined them saying over their forks while I tussled with a piece of meat. In truth, I probably did prod and probe the food a bit. By nature I harbour the inclination to treat everything as suspect until a friend or foe label is confirmed. It must have appeared rude and it's more likely they were saying, 'Look at the spoilt Irish bastard. If he'd gone through two wars and two occupations he'd be eating shite off a brush and be thankful for it too.'

The majority of Polish food, much like Irish food, is derived from peasant culture, where you pull what is available out of the ground or running along its surface and fling it into the pot. I would have to say, though, that the Poles are more imaginative than the Irish when it comes to creating dishes of this nature. Most of what went into the boarding school pot was delivered daily by horse and cart. And I was right about the horse. It had a massive pair of blinkers and a shaggy coat and stood deathly still,

every day, through every season, at the back of the kitchens while its master was inside 'nudge-nudging' with the
women. Thankfully, the horse remained alive for the
duration of my spell, otherwise paranoia would have
driven me as far away from that kitchen as possible.

The dining area was open between six and seven in
the morning for breakfast, twelve-thirty to three for
dinner and six to seven in the evening for tea, and was
worked by several friendly but sturdy women in the
kitchens, visible through the food hatches.

The hatches themselves were manned by the students
who stayed at the internat, and who operated a rota
system for dishing up the meals. In fact, the kids played a
very active role in all the schools and had a variety of
duties and responsibilities to contend with, all bearing a
distinctly communist hallmark. Without condoning the
system, I could see that it worked. The schools had a real
sense of order about them.

The roles of the students ranged from cooking, washing and cleaning to door duty. Any door really. Students
were stationed at the main doors of the school to check
IDs; at the doors of the internat to do likewise; at the toilet
doors; and even in the classrooms. Schools here, particularly girls' schools, suffer a fair amount from vagrants drifting in and out and peeping through windows. Anyone
who enters must show their official ID, which displays
their name, address and their profession. If they are students it will say what level they are – primary, secondary

or third level – and what institution they are attending. Big Brother is very much present, but he does stop the louts jumping in and out of the schoolgirls' beds – at least when they're in the school.

In the dining room, when you approached the first hatch you would be greeted by one of the kids with a large ladle in her hand guarding a massive cauldron of soup. After a polite 'hello', the ladle would descend into the depths of the pot with a rather unpleasant sound, like a Wellington boot in a puddle of mud. Once you collected your bowl of soup you moved on to the next hatch for a plate of food and a mug of tea with no handles, which you sort of gripped like a builder. The tea was black and already contained sugar. There was no milk.

For some reason, you were only ever given a fork, and had to chop with this as well as eat with it. It was a bit baffling. On the first day, when I had dinner with the director, I stood and went looking for a knife. Realising that there were none, I sat down and chopped with the side of the fork, chasing stragglers that were left around the plate with the thumb of my other hand. It felt a bit primitive, but nobody batted an eyelid. When you were finished your dinner, you brought the dishes up to a third hatch, where the cleaning was done.

As for the meals, well, the soup was usually a safe bet and was really a meal in itself. Now and then you'd find odd things in it, like half a carrot, a lump of turnip the size of a boot-heel, or even a boiled egg. Given the eye-like nature of a boiled egg, it is actually quite frightening to find one in your soup. It has a certain foreboding weight when you first go to lift it on the spoon and when it surfaces it's like you're being watched. But in general, the soup was good.

The main dish, however, was a gamble at the best of times. There were days in the beginning when I span on my heel like a ballerina, having caught sight of it early enough. Pasta with white cheese and sugar was one dish; lettuce with sour milk was a side salad, as was salad made from beetroot, an unsettling mound of purple gunk which I nicknamed 'afterbirth' and could never face again as a result; cutlets, made from minced pork, which were actually really good; minced pork again, this time wrapped in a cabbage leaf and sealed at both ends to form a sort of soggy sausage, which I called 'loathsome larvae', was a rather tasty dish too; and finally 'flaki', which looked like tapeworm but was actually the lining of a sheep's stomach. Tripe, I think my grandmother called it.

Most of these dishes were served with mashed potato containing strange foreign bodies of dubious colour, but at least the potato was, on the whole, familiar. Every meal was accompanied by small pickled cucumbers, which I went on to call 'slugs'.

The supper was okay – bread, boiled egg, ham or sausage, all served with a mug of black tea straight from a large plastic bucket – but I rarely bothered. I think it was the slosh of that tea-bucket that finally turned me off the supper. It had a prison ring to it that did my imagination no good.

Breakfast saw the return of the slop-out tea-bucket, along with bread, more boiled eggs and sausage. The sausages, incidentally, were those big mothers, the size of a policeman's truncheon. When you cooked them on a pan, you could grease the axle of a combine harvester with the amount of fat that was left behind. Very tasty, but no prizes for guessing why there's a serious problem with heart disease here.

Of course, once on the plate there was little you could do but eat whatever it was, or face the wrath of the largest of the women in the kitchens. One in particular kept a beady eye on the third hatch and observed the plates coming back with alarming alacrity. A large woman with a blue apron and beefy red arms, if my plate wasn't cleared, out she'd come and point at me, then down to my plate, throwing her hands in the air as if apologising to the Lord for the wanton waste of good food. Then she'd stare at my face and pull at her cheekbones, clearly implying that I was a skinny little bastard and needed every scrap before winter fell. It was all in jest of course, and she was a very kindly old soul, but with gangs of laughing kids at the tables behind me it didn't do much for my confidence. I always did my best to get the food down, or if it was really too bad I'd hide it in the plant pots beside the tables. I eventually decided to pretty much steer clear of the place altogether and take my chances in the shops.

Another area of the boarding building I learned to give a wide berth to was the main laundry room. This was located down in the basements. To get to it you had to descend a dark and very steep set of stairs, dropping so precipitously that you really had to sidle down tentatively sideways, like a crab. There in the steamy depths was where all the laundry for the boarding school was done, everything from sheets and blankets to the cooks' aprons, clothing, rugs, the lot. The job was left to one old woman, who toiled daily at massive machines that hissed and steamed and together created a room temperature of about thirty degrees Celsius. It reminded me of ghastly scenes in movies about Russian submarines. I didn't envy the poor woman, but neither was I quite sure what to make of her. My doubts were more from ignorance than anything else.

As a guest I was invited to have my clothes and sheets washed there once a week. So every Friday morning, with some trepidation, I'd descend those steps to face the mood swings of this woman, who either smiled graciously or tutted and swore and muttered under her breath as she inspected my clothing. This went on for a couple of weeks, until I decided that it just wasn't worth it. It was much later that I realised the poor woman was only being paid a pittance each month, and a simple tip of a couple of quid from me – even as a token of appreciation – would have meant the world. It honestly never occurred to me. I thought that my clothes were just part of her job but, as it turned out, I was an extra workload for her – one that, I'm sure, she could very easily have done without.

Since laundries didn't exist in the town, the substitute for the steamy basement was my bath. I filled it with hot water and detergent every Friday, dumped the dirty clothes in and stirred for twenty minutes with the handle of the sweeping brush. I'd leave them there until Saturday morning, rinse them with cold water, then take the lot out and hang them over the bath to dry. When strange rashes began to appear on my skin I realised that the rinsing process wasn't really working. So I asked the guys on the corridor how they washed their clothes.

They led me into the washroom, where a contraption like a metal bin stood near a drain. The top of this machine was open and, near the bottom, a short hose with a hook on the end of it jutted out like a small ele-phant's trunk. One of the guys grabbed the hose and, with the aid of the hook, fixed it to the top of the machine. Then he picked up a bucket and filled it with water, pour-ing the contents in at the open top. This was done several times, until the machine was almost full. Then he plugged it in. Considering the plug had been languishing on the soaking wet floor the whole time, I was quite happy to let him plug it in instead of me.

Suddenly the machine jumped to life, gyrating on the floor until a little whirlpool appeared in the water at the top. You simply threw in your powder and clothes, and that was that. It was a fairly primitive gadget, but more primitive still was the method of emptying the machine once the clothes were washed. There was no timer. You stuck your head in the door every now and again and checked the water. When it was dirty, you unplugged the machine, unhooked the hose and stood well back, unleashing a deluge of water out onto the floor. To rinse the clothes you repeated the above without adding detergent. After a few weeks of this frightening caper, I went back to the bath. You needed waders for the duration of the operation and anyway, I was sure that plug had my name on it.

There was, however, a sense of adventure attached to everyday chores that I began to enjoy. Everything had to be worked for. Convenience was a rarity. If you wanted to, you could fill your day with enough tasks that even thinking about it all would be a job in itself. At the same time, I knew that it would eventually become pure tedium and that then the thrill of being somewhere new might easily wear off. That thinking up new plans to teach the kids, who I loved, would become just another job. That dodging the kitchens and searching the shops for food would become a nightmare. That the view from the window would eventually become dull, and that I'd even get sick and tired of myself.

To Market, To Market

The older of the English teachers has a bad habit of staring at me when I come into the staff room in the mornings. She makes me say, 'Dzien dobry,' (good morning) several times over, much to the amusement of the staff. Also, like the woman in the kitchens, she pokes at my face regularly, indicating that I'm getting thin. She is clearly possessed of that mothering instinct that is particularly frustrating when you're trying to be independent. She tells me repeatedly about her son, who has since left town and who looks just like me. She is also obsessed with English grammar. Between lessons she nabs me in the staff room with several passages scribbled on bits of paper.

'Tom, I have some questions for you,' she says, tugging on my sleeves. 'Which is better and why? "Have you ever read *Wuthering Heights?*" Or, "Did you read *Wuthering Heights?*" How about, "I was in France three times," or, "I have been to France three times?"'

This is the nightmare I had envisioned, the questions that would freeze the bowels. As her stare becomes more intense, I nod with an air of professionalism, telling her I am late for a lesson and I will explain in detail later. Giving the kids a fifteen-minute assignment in class, I sift through the grammar handbook to find her answers. I finally avoided the staff room as much as possible, particularly when I knew this English teacher would be there. She was beginning to stray away from questions of grammar and onto more general ones about my educational background. I was terrified that one day I'd be exposed as a fraud.

I simply couldn't look bad in the staff room. There were rumours going around that I was an 'expert' and so I was somehow put on a pedestal. The fact that I only had a BA degree and had legged it over there with a half-written Master's thesis was a constant burden that I often felt compelled to confess. It was probably a good thing in the end, since it forced me to complete that thesis. It filled those dark, lonely hours when winter came tapping on the window and the mind needed any kind of food it could get its hands on.

To become a teacher in Poland you have to have a Master's degree in your chosen subject. On top of that, teachers have to spend several years at the bottom of the salary ladder, until they've earned their stripes. So, to instil a further sense of guilt, I entered the school passing myself off as a fully qualified and experienced teacher, with a Master's degree and in receipt of a full salary.

The salary was actually paltry, about one hundred pounds a month. Pay day, though, despite the humble pay packet, was still a day of high spirits for us all. The last Friday of every month, all the teachers would file down to the bursar's office and be handed a huge wad of money, about five million zloty. I was paid about two hundred pounds a month extra by APSO, so the school cash, which we termed 'Monopoly money', would all have finished up in the bar tills of Warsaw by that Sunday. But when I thought about it, there were teachers there with families, who had to feed kids and pay bills out of that measly wage. Poland was cheap, sure, but it would still have been a great struggle to stretch that money out.

The English teacher was, however, an exceptionally kind woman and anxious to see that I settled in, both around the town and in the school. In the beginning, I don't know what I would have done without her, as I was, quite frankly, lost. This was a town that had no means of coping with a foreigner. The general response when trying to purchase something in a shop, for example, was either benign confusion or an abrupt grunt, unless you had something at least written in Polish to indicate what you wanted. If truth be told, for every question this woman had for me, I had about five in return. And by the time a couple of weeks were out, I had a list of things that I badly needed but had no idea where to find. Books for school, painkillers, a few new shirts, a slice for the frying pan, a toilet brush, a welcome mat for myself at the front door – those small items that would make life a little bit easier. I approached her with this list and she immediately arranged a day to bring me around parts of the town that I hadn't yet discovered, beginning with the local market.

The market in the town was clearly the place to go. A great big bustling funfair, you could hear it long before it came into view. Here you could get everything you wanted, provided fashion wasn't on your list of priorities and, when it came to the derivation of foodstuffs, curiosity wasn't in your nature. Shirts and trousers that would have struck smiles of nostalgia on the faces of the Bay City Rollers were sold from the backs of trucks and carts. Giant, muddy vegetables in cloth sacks were heaped into huge weighing scales. In what seemed nothing more than primitive sheds, lumps of meat were being severed and split by an intimidating array of weaponry in the capable hands of the Polish butchers.

It was a lively, colourful place, but we had picked a bad day to go. Being muggy and wet, the ground beneath was a sea of mud. Occasionally a horse would invigorate the cold air with a rasping fart that mingled with the smells of feet, rotten vegetables, wet muck and alcohol. Eventually, after a couple of rounds of ogling, we began to barter with a man selling shirts and slacks from a stall. I bought a pair of black trousers and two shirts with wing-like collars and a sort of flecky pattern, just so we could leave the bedlam behind us. I can't remember how much I paid for them, but I do remember that I never wore them. We managed to pick up a few of the other items on my list, however, so it was a reasonably fruitful forage overall.

After the market, we moved on to a couple of small stores where I got hold of a few more bits and pieces, stores that gave no indication that they were stores at all and could only be known through local knowledge. Tiny stores here specialised in the oddest things – shoe-laces, batteries, wrapping paper – and how the people made a living from such wares was anyone's guess. What would happen to them when the chain stores and supermarkets moved in – and they would – was a more depressing prospect still, even if it would prove to be more expedient.

But from all the stores we visited that day I found only one that had foolscap paper. I needed mounds of it, because I had made the decision to complete my half-written thesis and, with no PC, would have to do it by hand. It made me feel like I had travelled back in time. By the end of that first year, I had on several occasions bought out all the foolscap stock in that one shop.

We also visited a couple of small bookstores, where I got hold of a dictionary, a chemist's for some drugs, and the church, of course, for a quick prayer. That afternoon I went to the woman's home to meet her mother, who was still alive but barely visible in a dark corner of the house. Bearing in mind that the teacher herself had retired, and was only doing a few hours' teaching a week to keep her occupied, I was baffled as to the age of her mother. I even wondered, considering the lack of movement from the dark corner that day, whether she really was alive at all and had visions of myself being cracked over the back of the head with a spade during lunch.

Giving me a tour of the rest of the house, my colleague told me to visit as often as I liked, adding that her home was my home and that I was always welcome. This offer, as I was to discover much later with other families, was not made merely through courtesy, but was perfectly genuine.

After lunch, she meandered inevitably onto the subject of my weight loss, before escorting me rather worryingly to the army barracks. Standing in the doorway of a building that seemed like a large banquet hall, she informed me that you could get breakfast, dinner and tea there for next to nothing. I couldn't for the life of me comprehend going to an army barracks for dinner, and it took me more than two years to pluck up the courage to try. But when I did I was astounded. For the equivalent of roughly two euro, you could get a full meal in a clean, warm and comfortable dining area at fixed times of the day. Families would arrive on a Sunday afternoon, or there might be people like myself, sitting alone to eat.

Usually there were two choices of menu, which included three courses – soup, a main course and a dessert. If you didn't fancy sitting in the main area you could head to the café/bar part, which I often did. The army officers used this area more frequently than the general public, and here light food, snacks and soups were available, as well as beer and vodka. There would almost always be a group of officers playing cards and sharing a bottle of vodka here, with a large jar of those slugs to chase it down. It would have been the perfect place to spend a Sunday afternoon reading a book and sipping a cold beer, only the air was so thick with the most pungent cigarette smoke, I'm surprised the officers even managed to tell the suits on the cards.

It was all part of the State service, and I soon discovered that soldiers – the common privates and raw conscripts at least – are in the same pool here as the lowest ranks of civil service or even the unemployed. It is the duty of a soldier to carry out a variety of local tasks that seem designed to make them feel worthless.

These tasks range from acting as doormen at the local hop to keeping the garden of an officer. Every year there is also the town clean-up, where students and their teachers traipse through the streets, across train tracks and into the woods with bags to collect rubbish. At various points around the town, soldiers serve pea soup from the backs of jeeps to give the cleaners energy. I went on this escapade one year, and while the clean-up was a bit grim, the steaming bowl of pea soup and bread in the cold afternoon was a joy.

On any day of national celebration – and there are many in Poland – the army is there for support and to serve up this pea soup. The soldiers, however, are a morose bunch who look seriously underfunded and often malnourished. They form a part of the general populace of a town, ambling about the streets aimlessly like stray pigeons. Brawls and loud swearing in the middle of the night can usually be put down to a drunken soldier, and you soon learn where the phrase 'smoke like a trooper' comes from. Ditto 'swear' and 'drink'.

Although the barracks eventually proved a better option than the internat for lunch, I was never able to thank this teacher for her tip. The following year she arrived on the first day to be told that she had no lessons. The poor woman was devastated. They never informed her that she was officially let go and she turned up for the opening ceremony, as she had done for God knows how many years, to find that this time her name was missing from the roster. I met her once after that and promised I'd visit her, but I never did. I never even saw her again before I left for good. It is easy to convince yourself that it was the fault of time, that you had gone too far to go back. When I'm old and grey, and forced to retire from whatever the hell I'm doing, I'm sure I'll remember that.

Skinned and Boned

I was getting thin. In fact, the pounds were falling off me like leaves in autumn. I hated taking a bath, because a glance in the bathroom mirror revealed a ribcage like the bellows on an accordion. There were also queries from the cooks as to why I wasn't coming down for dinner and tea every day, communicated to me via the director, via one of the other English teachers. They were concerned for my well-being, as was anyone else who caught a glance at me. I told them that I had different eating habits, preferring a big dinner in the evening and a light lunch in the afternoon. They didn't really buy it, so I went for the odd dinner on a Thursday when I figured out it was 'meat' day.

I had got that information from some of the kids in school. I began to notice that the boarding students in the 12.30 class on Thursdays were always itching to leave early. They would look at their watches constantly and whisper to each other in the last quarter of the class. This was one of the 'post maturity' classes, so I wasn't all that surprised. But one day, with a badly planned lesson and twenty minutes left over at the end, I began to chat idly with them about the school, the internat and the general trials of life around the town.

They had all kinds of complaints, most of which had never occurred to me – curfews, cleaning duties, cold rooms, cockroaches, irregular hot water and skimpy bedclothes. It was some eye-opener, and I think they detected my fear when the cockroaches were mentioned. I can tolerate many things, but not insects, and especially not cockroaches.

I knew it was only a matter of time before the inevitable occurred. One evening, I came into my kitchen and turned on the light, to see scores of insects tearing across the floor like a scatter of marbles. I didn't get a wink of sleep, but spent the night flicking the light on and off and looking under the sheets. At first light I went to the director with the English teachers in tow as interpreters. I told him that if something wasn't done lickety-split, I was either going home or to a hotel in Warsaw. As it turned out, the director of the internat had ordered the whole building fumigated – every inch of it, except my flat, which made a huge amount of sense. The roaches, which are pretty adept at survival, realised there was one safe corner left in the building, and promptly moved in with me.

Eventually, the fumigator was recalled and I had to vacate the place for the weekend. The only thing I had to worry about thereafter was the state of my lungs, wondering what the hell the guy had used in my flat. I never saw so many creatures on their backs in all my life. It was a fairly unnerving experience, but I was not alone. One of the other Irish guys, Gearoid, a big lad from Cork, had a worse deal when it came to the roaches.

He had been placed in a town called Miedzyrzec Podlaski, further east. I passed through it once and remember being glad that I was only passing through. You could tell how bad our various towns were by the number of times we visited each other, and I don't think anyone ever visited Gearoid. Back when we had arrived at the monastery in the summer, almost all of us had our accommodation set up, but there were a couple of people who still had no confirmed home and the APSO project manager was trying to sort them out. Gearoid was told one day that he had a choice regarding his accommodation – he could share with a family or live in a workers' hostel that, in the words of the project manager, 'you wouldn't put a dog in'. Of course, he opted for the family. When the shared arrangement wasn't working out he tried to find somewhere else, but APSO were slow to move on it back in Dublin, so he just went to the hostel himself.

Several months later, when the project manager was over again on a sort of assessment mission, he asked Gearoid how things were with the family. Gearoid told him he'd since moved out. 'To where?' asked our manager. 'To the place you wouldn't put a dog in,' answered Gearoid.

One can only imagine what it was like. There, he said, roaches crawled regularly from a drain in the corridor. Gearoid poured every chemical available, from bleach to vodka, into the throat of the drain, hoping it would discourage the roaches from surfacing. But it only made things worse, since he swore they began to mutate. Large roaches with several antennae, three legs and other deformities began haunting him nightly. I was never sure whether to believe him or not though, as he had grown quite fond of pouring a variety of stuff down his own throat by then.

After my chat with the students that day, I realised that I clearly had a better deal than some. But there were a few things that we had in common. The building we shared was definitely cold – when the wind blew at night, the windows sang like panpipes. And this was still autumn. The rain came in under the cracked window panes, but I knew that from the first week here and had blocked the main points of entry with towels. At one stage however, the whole frame – containing three separate windows – came in on top of me when I recklessly tried to force open a window that had refused to budge since my arrival. I was left standing in a crucifixion pose holding the windows for some time, until I could secure it and go for help. That evening the school carpenter arrived, with a little cotton bag of nails around his shoulder and a hammer stuck in his belt like a gunslinger.

He was an old man and walked with a bit of a limp, frowning when he saw that the whole window frame had simply popped out like a large eye. But it didn't take him long to remedy the matter. A few nails, a few whacks of the hammer and a firm nod. That was that sorted for the coming winter.

I felt for the poor kids, particularly with regard to the cold. Between the windows and the central heating system, which ran off a massive coal-burning boiler but whose coal was spared for only the coldest days, the internat was not always warm. At least I had an electric heater, bought for me after a teacher leaked the information that I was taking the hob cooker out of the kitchen and into the main bedroom every night to get a bit of extra heat. The brand spanking new electric heater that arrived at my door made a good bit of difference. It also blew fuses regularly. The fuse box for the whole corridor, one of those antiquated boards with huge, ceramic fuses rather than trip switches, was in my hallway. Before a fuse blew there would be an ominous and quite frightening fizzling sound, like a giant glass of coke being poured out in the hall. Then bang. Lights out, electric heater out, the lot.

All I could do was enjoy the darkness and wait until the following day to summon the school electrician. He would arrive in his blue coat, approaching the fuse box with the caution of a soldier about to defuse a landmine. Extracting the old fuse carefully, he would replace it with another as large as the butt of a snooker cue. Then, with a short smile, he would leave. Within three days he would be back to do it all over again. We became very close, that electrician and I.

But the worst gripe I had in common with the students concerned the food. The only good day was Thursday, because you got meat, and to get the best bits you had to be there early. As for the food in general, they shrugged indifferently. We went through the menu of the various days together. What I thought I was eating, and what they told me I was eating, were two very different things, except for the sheep's stomach. I was right about that – it was sheep's stomach all right, and none of them liked it. But they ate it. That was the difference. It was food, and they were hungry all the time.

One evening, some of the older guys who lived in the block came to my flat looking for bread. Most likely it was simply to accompany the vodka they had managed to smuggle in, but it was still pretty alarming. They treated bread as if it were actually manna from heaven. Whatever else you found in bins here if you went looking, you'd rarely find a piece of bread. From then on, I let them go early on Thursday and we all got the best bits of meat together.

People underestimate the importance of food. When it is there in front of you all the time it doesn't have a real value. But I grew to respect food greatly that first year, knowing that it would make the difference between me coming home to Ma looking like Dracula, a beanpole or – God forbid – in a black body bag. I was reminded often enough that I was getting close to one of these. Obtaining food, however, was the greatest of inconveniences.

The supermarket in a small town would generally only have basic goods. The shop could be full, but there would be nothing there to eat. You could find pasta in every form imaginable, tins of odd stuff, single frozen fish gazing up at you with glassy eyes, and packets of that noodle soup they give out free in student unions. Getting a meal of decent food together meant visiting the grocer, the butcher, the baker and so on, accumulating all your ingredients and rolling up your sleeves for an evening bent over the hob.

Most of the time I just wasn't bothered, and arrived home to make do with whatever I'd come up with in one shop. Usually that was soup of some sort, normally powdered stuff, accompanied by bread. I ate barrels of this desiccated rubbish. When I later grew more adroit at the language, I realised it was sauce I had been eating, and not soup. Whatever it was, I knew it wasn't much use. It filled rather than nourished, and my final belch lacked substance, suggesting that little had passed through my body but hot water. Christ, I was starving in those days.

Vegetables were okay when you could get them. They sat in big baskets on the floor of the grocer's shop. But in winter they were harder to come by and, as they were caked with frozen muck, it was hard to distinguish between them. They were all just brown – beetroots, potatoes, turnips, all just brown lumps. At least you could tell a carrot from its shape.

Meat was almost always bought on the bone, which meant having to hack it up yourself. If you wanted a couple of pork chops, you were shown the full spine of a pig. You indicated how much you wanted and an axe was promptly cracked down on the bone. Coming home with half a pig's back wrapped in newspaper does nothing for the appetite. Sawing through it with a penknife is particularly unappealing. But asking the butcher to do it for you was the greatest of all evils in Poland. The butchers, for some reason, felt they had done enough once the beast was swinging in the window. What you did with it after that was none of their business.

Having visited all the butchers in my town, I eventually gave them separate titles, to amuse myself. There was Butcher Nice, Butcher Nasty, Butcher Nervy and, finally, Butcher Nephritis. So, here goes:

Butcher Nice is a big, broad lump of a woman with a small but profitable business among the locals. She greets you with a smile as large as a rasher and almost always gives you a few 'extras', with a wink and a sly grin. I imagine that, although her trade dictates it, she weeps nightly at the slaughter of all the poor animals that go under her knife. I even suspect she keeps a pet cemetery hidden away in the orchard somewhere, memorials of all the beasts sent to the great butcher shop in the sky. She is my favourite of the quartet, and the one most likely to win an award. Although she does oblige when you ask her to cut up the meat, this is the shop with the biggest queue, so I don't visit it as often as I would like. The word for 'cut' in Polish is a bit of a tongue-twister, not worth risking in front of the natives.

By contrast – and what a contrast – comes Butcher Nasty, who works in the 'delicatessy' that I visit the most. This woman is to animals what Satan is to God-fearing Christians. Mean and tight and with a stare that would stop a cuckoo emerging from its clock, she cuts cold meats using a cheese-wire and a ruler. I recall one day when I wanted to buy a chicken breast, but being so nervous in her presence mistakenly asked for a chicken instead. When she came out with a whole, freshly slaughtered fowl, I apologised and pointed to the breasts sitting on the tray. The torrent of abuse I received nearly made me wet my pants with fright. I only once requested that she cut the pig's back into chops for me, and never did so again. She wrapped them in a newspaper with the headline 'Murder' on one of the pages, and followed me with her eyes when I was leaving the shop.

Next up is Butcher Nervy, who has to be watched carefully. Butcher Nervy is a schizophrenic. Although she works alone, I distinctly heard her talking to her 'assistant' one day when I asked for a pound of sausages. She also gave me a pile of dodgy ribs and when I brought them back she blamed her 'assistant', telling me she would be severely punished. The type of character that would have floated around the mind of Hitchcock, Butcher Nervy wields the knife in a callous and brutal, yet disturbingly calm, manner, hacking away at the meat like a dysfunctional schoolboy dissecting a frog. The meat she gives out tends to vary in colour when cooked – a bit like those rainbow gobstoppers you ate as a kid – and I often have guessing games as to whether it originated on the ground, in the sky or even in the sea. Still, she's not the worst of them.

That prize goes to Butcher Nephritis. Nephritis is, of course, a digestive disorder, in the gallery of disorders like colic, botulism, flatulence, piles, ulcers, gripes and so on. Mysterious visits to the toilet in the middle of the night can only be a result of Butcher Nephritis and her handiwork. Again, it's a difficult one to prove, but I have a gut feeling about it, as they say. Butcher Nephritis' shop looks and smells like a lepers' graveyard. But Butcher Nephritis is really a kindly old soul, a typical country butcher, and perhaps only for this have the tools of her trade not been confiscated and herself locked away in a walk-in freezer for a minimum sentence of ten years.

What did I survive on? As time went on, things got better. Some of the shops even began to bring in self-service – like that delicatessy, for example. No more queues! The town was transformed, but over the course of years, not weeks or months. Occasionally, I would strike gold in this delicatessy store – perhaps discovering some tinned beans in tomato sauce, a rare and valued commodity. I also ate a lot of eggs, fresh as daisies, many still decorated with feathers and gick. However, concerned for my cholesterol level, I eventually cut back a bit on my egg consumption. As for milk, the milk you could get in cartons here was UHT – you couldn't drink it straight or you'd be as sick as a pike. I tried drinking two cartons a day when I was told I was losing weight and began to grow extremely pale, developing huge circles like eclipses of the moon under my eyes. If you wanted 'fresh' milk, you were really taking your life into your own hands. Fresh milk, until EU hygiene tests came in, was never pasteurised and came in plastic bags. Putting milk in a plastic bag is an idea that must have flown straight past the main door of the logic department. You hold the bag under your elbow and cut the corner off it with a scissors and the stuff shoots out all over the table. I mean, have the Poles never come across bagpipes?

The milk was dodgy stuff anyway, causing ripples in the bowels. It failed all the EU hygiene tests when they were eventually initiated, despite the fact that one farmer proclaimed, 'What's wrong with it? You can see with the naked eye that it's perfectly all right.'

I ate hamburgers for a while, until I began to feel unwell. At fifty pence for ten I wasn't too surprised. They were made from tails, bones and teeth. I know that's a fact, because a friend of mine worked in an abattoir and told me that whatever was left on the floor at the end of the day went into the burgers. Feeling another animal's tooth in your gob is an experience that lifts your hair by the root. *You're* supposed to be eating *it*.

My suspicions regarding the meat would later be confirmed. In 2003, prior to EU accession, the European Commission warned Poland about standards at meat processing plants. Only sixty-six of the country's 3,300 red meat plants were passed and given permits to export their produce within the rest of Europe. I survived anyway, so I must have been getting my meat from one of those sixty-six.

Vodka Crush

Thankfully, the chance came after a couple of months to sample a real cooked meal in a Polish restaurant. Teachers' Day had come around. It is a communist tradition to have days held aside to honour anyone and everyone, from teachers and doctors to mothers and their children. It keeps them all happy, giving everyone something to celebrate, and is used as a general distraction from more serious concerns.

Teachers' Day was a pleasant surprise for me that first year, as representatives from all the classes presented me with flowers, chocolates or bottles of beer. It was a fairly moving experience, since I wasn't used to being given flowers. Of course, other teachers got flowers as well, but not all. I realised that day that a teacher's popularity with the kids could be gauged by the amount of flowers they received on Teachers' Day.

As well as receiving flowers from the students and some small financial prizes from the State, it is a custom for teachers to go out together and get lashed. Now, I didn't know the social habits of Poles the first year. I was simply told that there was an evening out for the teachers and that a table was booked in the local 'zajazd' for six o'clock. A 'zajazd' is a type of guesthouse, found more often in the countryside than in larger towns. Warm, comfortable, typically Polish buildings with a bit of character, they serve food and drink all night until the last guest topples. This particular place was located on the edge of town and was fairly popular until the 'mafia' took over.

The 'mafia' are really just local thugs. They like to go by the name of 'mafia', since it adds a sense of import. Usually operating in small gangs, they earn their living in markets, as well as by theft. They are worth keeping away from since they're essentially brain dead, and would be unable to comprehend the existence of a foreigner in their locale. Their reaction to something perplexing would probably be to stab it.

Hearing a table is booked, I decide to avoid food all day, savouring instead the prospect of a fine cooked dinner. Before leaving, I sit with a beer in my flat, picturing festoons of large sausages and steak, dirty big mounds of dumplings, big wads of sour cabbage, gravy thick as porter and tankards of frothy beer, all the trimmings that my imagination had conjured up back in Dublin.

Putting on my best clothes, I arrive after six to find a table of about fifteen teachers gathered around enough vodka to kill an army and barely a morsel of food to mop it up with. The 'menu', I am told, has been set. My reaction swings from alarm to bitter disappointment, before finally settling on the primitive urge to escape. Too late.

Before I have time to say, 'I'd murder a bloody burger and fries,' I am planted at the table and a shot of vodka is pushed into the palm of my hand.

It is a general rule in situations of survival to eat anything that swims, walks or flies, as long as it has been cooked. Many vegetarians would be disgusted at that statement, but to be a vegetarian in Poland is a luxury that most people simply can't afford. It is very hard to get fresh fruit and vegetables, especially in winter, and it is also quite expensive. You eat what is put in front of you, whether from the air, the ground or the sea. As long as it's not pink, I'll give it a try.

On this night, for the first course we have raw herring in oil. A hideous-looking scrap, it slips down the throat like a badly bruised banana, to be chased by a two-ounce shot of vodka, as is customary. The result is a rapid wrenching of the gut, together with temporary lockjaw to prevent it from coming back up. The taste itself beggars description.

The second course is 'tatar', a serious disappointment, having starved all day for it. Tatar, I am told proudly, is a 'typical delicacy', consisting of raw, minced beef mashed with raw onion and crowned with the yoke of a raw egg. It strikes the fear of God in me. I later learn that God was right to have struck fear in me, as I am told of a man who got a tapeworm from the stuff. I push it away, only to be warned that I will be held upside down and force-fed by the PE teacher if I don't eat it.

I glance at the PE teacher. He is a nice guy, but big, a sort of gentle giant. He has been mixing the 'cocktails' all night – cocktails merely being shots of vodka and orange juice, but he calls them cocktails and he looks pretty serious. With the aid of handfuls of bread, bits of cake and straight vodka to kill off any tapeworms, I manage to get through half of the tatar. The remainder goes into the pocket of my suit.

A couple of hours later, a good ten bottles of vodka have been put away. I go and buy another one for the table as a sort of gesture. Nobody gives a shite. It is opened and gone again in twenty minutes.

The pace of the drinking is astounding. I was never a vodka drinker and if I ever drank it, it was with a mixer and sipped. So, if your evening consisted of five vodkas, there would be five bottles of minerals as partners. Here, the mixer is used as a chaser only, and a mouthful at that. A shot is poured and downed in one go, followed by a quick gulp of mineral to wash it back, and so an entirely disparate ratio applies. You could have five shots of vodka in an hour, and only one glass of mixer. Those slugs are eaten as chasers also, and jars of them sit around the table along with the plates of herring and tatar. In fact, between all the raw material here, the table resembles some sort of gruesome science lab.

As the evening continues and the table inevitably breaks up into smaller gatherings, I am left beside the PE teacher, who pours vodka into my glass at regular fifteen-minute intervals. He can't speak English and I can't speak Polish, but the universal tongue between us here is drink. Together we engage in a lengthy dialogue ending in inebriated pickings at scraps of food, cooked or not.

Come midnight, the singing starts. I am in the land of oblivion and holding hands for some reason with the teacher beside me, a young woman who is rocking sideways to the rhythm as she sings. She is a really decent girl who works as duty officer in the internat and to whom I go for domestic assistance the most. It is all a bit of gas but I'm not sure the rocking is a good idea. Suddenly, she leans forward and grabs the bottom of the tablecloth in a rather nugatory attempt to catch a load of herring and raw steak, surfing on a wave of vodka. It is a grim sight and a worse smell, and between the two a dampener descends on the occasion. Curtains then for that party. But at least I can now look the teachers in the eye without the timid smile of the outsider. Having drank and held down the best part of a bottle of vodka as well as a variety of recently deceased animals, I have earned it.

The next day I decide that vodka is a strange drink. I'm not hungover in the traditional sense. No headache; my stomach is numb but holding its own and I can focus reasonably well. I feel, though, like I'm in another dimension to the rest of the world outside, as if stuck inside a large wooden barrel or the belly of a whale. Sounds take their time getting through. Thoughts seem unable to develop. There is a fog there that doesn't seem like lifting. I am also bled of the volition to do anything except lie on my back and stare at the ceiling. It is akin to the type of punishment you might read about in the Old Testament, where God was a cruel bugger with a dark sense of humour.

The vodka hangover also causes the sufferer to experience negative feelings such as doubt, guilt, inadequacy, fear and forgetfulness. I use the term forgetfulness rather than loss of memory, because there is a distinction. Loss of memory can be permanent, or at least for a prolonged period of time. With forgetfulness, bad experiences come flooding back over the course of the day like slaps in the face. It is as if I had transformed into a werewolf the previous night and have woken up staring at my hands, wondering what the hell I got up to, and knowing that it is only a matter of time before I remember.

And there is something else I've noticed. For the first time since getting here, I am actually terribly depressed and feel completely abandoned. It is Friday, so at least I don't have to get up early and teach. But I am gripped by a very bleak humour, which doesn't actually have a cause, even though I spend the whole morning looking for one. Nothing is more depressing than not having a reason for being depressed. I have a feeling it is going to happen a lot here. It is the vodka, and this doesn't bode well. From what I have seen so far, bread, vodka and those awful slugs are the Holy Trinity in this country. I will just have to conform.

As for the loneliness, there isn't a lot I can do about it.

Because of the poor telecommunications system in the region, correspondence with the other Irish teachers is generally by postcard, stating a date and a place to meet – usually a bar in Warsaw. There is always an anxious moment on Friday mornings, when you stick your head into the staff room to see if there is a card or not.

The phone numbers we have are unreliable at the best of times. Take Paul, in that village of Sadowne. He is so isolated that to contact him I have to go to the post office and hand the girl at the counter the number on a piece of paper, then take a seat. She contacts Warsaw central, who contact the post office in Sadowne, who in turn contact his school. It can take up to half an hour, and then I am suddenly told to go into one of the booths, that the call has come through. More often than not I simply get a voice saying, 'Paul, nie ma.' What this means is another weekend alone in the flat. I am beginning to hate that phrase.

It All Comes Down
to Buttons

I was right to worry about winter. It arrived quite suddenly one morning at the end of October, like somebody had just tipped it out of a cardboard box overnight. My first reaction was to look at the thermometer to see how cold it was, then write home to everyone and gather a bit of sympathy, as well as some awe.

'Lads, it's bloody freezing here. It's so cold in fact that when I have a shower my hair freezes on the way to school.' Then the parcels started arriving. I got a thermal scarf from Ma, a World Cup video from Dad, Marks & Spencer's pre-packed dinners from my aunt in London and a package of magic mushrooms from a friend in Wicklow. I don't know what condition he thought I was in to send me that. But the Marks and Sparks dinners, which I heated in a pot of boiling water, drooling just at the smell of the steam, were a joy.

The novelty of the snow in Poland lasts about a day. After a few fleeting snowball fights and a couple of snowmen, people simply knuckle down to the prospect of a long winter ahead. It is long and it can be bitterly cold.

Temperatures throughout the winter season, which runs roughly from the end of October to any time around March, can range from two or three degrees Celsius on a good day to minus twenty or less. In general, the temperature barely rises above the minus-eight mark.

The worst thing about the cold, however, is the monotony it brings in its wake. It is dark all the time, or at least it seems that way. Everyday chores become a bore as you notice things taking longer. There's a reluctance to get out of bed in the morning when you can sense how cold it is on your toes. Once up you dive for the bath. Getting out of the bath onto the cold screed floor is even more difficult than getting out of bed. There are all the extra layers of clothes to put on. Once outside the warmth of the building, the cold air bites your bones and pierces your lungs. You hesitate to go out at all most days.

The streets are like ice rinks and you have to stare at your feet with every pace. Kids whizz past on homemade sleds and you swear at them like an old man. Balance was never my strong point and I have a feeling I will come to dread walking here in winter. Because you have to visit various shops to buy various things – something I had started getting used to – the daily trip involves lumbering along dark, glassy streets and pavements, from one end of town to the other, walking like a bloody penguin.

Gradually, and in stark contrast to myself, I begin to notice that the people here are as tough as nails. There are no stoppages. Not unless the temperatures drop to minus forty degrees will the general daily services grind to a halt. Otherwise, there are no excuses for closing schools or being late for work. Poles keep their heads down and get on with their lives.

You hear the evidence at the start of every day when you're tucked up under a bundle of blankets. At five-thirty each morning, out come the 'scrapers', as I call them. A long piece of wood for a handle, with a thin, square section of plywood on the end, is the tool of their trade. Most people look after the area in front of their own homes, but in a school, hospital or any State institution there are people who get up in the darkness to scrape the snow from the paths and the steps. The noise is incredible and, as it snows later on anyway, it doesn't always do much good. In fact, if it doesn't snow it actually makes things worse, since the thin layer of snow left after the scrapers have done their job becomes smooth from people's boots and as hard as polished marble. Everyone goes on their arse at some stage. I just hope that when I land on mine, I do it in private behind a bush or some place. I couldn't face the humiliation of it in front of the school windows.

I am, however, thankful for at least having the basic utilities to hand. Most people, when you mention Poland, or any other former communist country, think 'grim, grey blocks', and conjure a mental picture of a family perched on a wooden bench, clutching a potato each and watching water bubbling in a pot. Which is accurate to a point. Post-war housing policy in Poland followed the Soviet model across the board. There are rustic wooden homes scattered across the countryside, but there was very little housing left in the major cities here after the war. The principle behind the Soviet model was that all housing was public property and a direct tool of the State's social policy. So the construction of private dwellings was forbidden. Private construction firms were also taken over by the State and contracted to build dwellings of standardised design. Low rents ensured that all citizens had a home, although, with concentration in the major urban areas, the rural areas tended to escape direct control. So you would see dismally constructed grey blocks in all the major cities, a clash of blocks and old wooden homes in suburban areas and, finally, the very quaint little wooden homes predominant in rural areas.

Under the communist regime, low rent, fuel, electricity and maintenance were, theoretically at any rate, accounted for, but the homes of peasants who remained 'free' would not have been well maintained by the State. So a lot of houses still exist in smaller towns and villages with no running water. Early in the morning, in freezing temperatures, you would see people walking down the street with a metal bucket to their local water pump.

The nearest pump to me was on a muddy laneway that served as a shortcut to the main street. This lane was visible from my window, and one morning I noticed an elderly woman arm-wrestling with the pump, which was stuck solidly beneath at least three inches of ice. In fact, if you weren't aware of the precise location of that pump, you would never have found it. Nothing but a sledgehammer in the arms of a lumberjack was going to free it. After several attempts the woman simply left, swinging an empty bucket. It occurred to me then how important that bucket of water must have been. Think about it – how many times a day do you need to turn on a tap? How much water do you need for drinking, cooking, washing clothes, washing your teeth? How many buckets of water does it take to fill a bath? Well, I'll give you an idea.

During the school 'winter' holiday, a period of two weeks in February, the hot water was turned off, and unless you made plans to be elsewhere, you had to grin and bear it. One year I didn't leave, and for the two weeks it was back to The Shining again – long, empty corridors, wind whistling through the windows and a few short hours of daylight that passed without notice. But the worst thing was trying to get the flat warm. The school boilers remained stoked up just enough to prevent burst pipes, but it was particularly cold. I remember one teacher, who had just moved into the internat before the holidays, looking fairly shell-shocked when I met him one evening. He remarked that it was 'very cold' in the building. If a Pole says it's 'very cold', then it must really be cold. You never hear Polish people complaining, unless they're seriously bowled over by something. If I had said it to him, I would have turned the air a far deeper shade of blue than it already was.

Getting to sleep wrapped in every item of clothing, hat and all, is easy enough, but waking up is a nightmare. Really unpleasant coldness has a particular presence in the room; there's a taut stillness in the air you're afraid might snap if you move. It feels like the Snow Queen has paid a visit and everything is frozen solid. Even the colour of the air changes – red for hot and blue for cold are uncannily accurate representations. Getting up eventually, I would put on a few more layers of clothing before switching on the radio, the two-ring cooker, the electric heater, the lights and the kettle. Everything was cold to the touch, but once some steam began to rise a certain lease of life would penetrate the sleeping flat. It was then that I would think about the bath and back to that question: How many buckets of water does it take to fill it?

The answer lies not in the capacity of the bath, but in how much water you're prepared to boil. You can have a decent wash in a tub with the water almost up to your navel, but you won't enjoy it, since you can't lie back. That takes about two hours of to-ing and fro-ing. In the beginning, when several pots have been emptied but are barely visible in the bottom of the bath, the magnitude of the task hits home. To have an enjoyable bath using a pot, a kettle and a two-ring stove, you need at least three hours. It was a great way of passing the time.

So, whenever I saw the inhabitants of the wooden houses clatter down the streets to the pumps with their metal buckets, that's what I thought about. Three hours of waiting. And most of them have large families. Lord knows what goes on there. The good thing is, three hours of steam will warm up your home.

The first year, besides some thermal 'long johns' and a pair of gloves, I wasn't very prepared for the cold, figuring that buying local was the best way. Even the thermal long johns I'd bought were useless – in school the radiators were pumping, so when you returned home, peeling the long johns from your bum was like prising open a clam.

Eventually, I ventured into Warsaw and bought a new coat, a massive, knee-length item with an interior of wool that was supposedly from a sheep and an exterior of monkey-brown-coloured suede. I thought it was a steal when I purchased it from the mountain folk who sell their wares – leather slippers, goats' cheese and hats with little flaps for your ears – on the corner of one of the main streets in Warsaw, near a restaurant called the London Steak House. The name of the restaurant stands out in my memory, because I was refused entry by a Victorian-looking butler once I'd put the new coat on. He scanned me from head to toe with the speed of a woodpecker before sticking an arm up and shaking his head. It was probably because the coat had no buttons and made me look like a nomad. I felt a fool then, but only half the fool I felt the following day in school, with the coat tied at the waist with a piece of string.

You imagine that if you dress like the locals you're going to blend in like a chameleon, but it doesn't work like that. People knew who I was wherever I went – in shops, in bars, on trains. Any attempt to look like everyone else only ever had the opposite effect. Anyhow, the coat was designed for 'Gorali', the mountain folk, and I soon gathered that I was the only person wearing one for hundreds of miles.

Polish people aren't afraid to laugh at you, and they don't bother to wait until you've walked round the corner – an admirable candour, I suppose. So I was faced with a choice between buying another coat and saving face, or getting a few buttons and taking the slagging on the chin. I went for the buttons, because I was broke. The coat had cost about a hundred quid and, while I was quite well-off relative to where I was, I was actually making little and saving nothing.

After several unsuccessful attempts at sewing the buttons on myself, I began asking people where I could have them done. A tailor, I was told in school. A tailor? Do they still exist? One of the teachers took me down a side road, where a few tailors worked in small shops. It seemed like a simple enough job, but no tailor would touch it, each one pointing out that a mistake would leave an irreparable gaping hole in the delicate suede.

I had already done that, which was probably another reason why they didn't want to tackle it. I had also tried to repair the hole by burning it with a match, figuring it would behave like nylon rope and fuse together. It didn't. So the whole thing was a bit of a mess. Finally, Jarek – the young guy who I'd met on the first day and was a reliable source of information – told me he knew somebody who might do it for me. And so, late one afternoon, we met up and began walking across town to an area I hadn't yet ventured into.

The reason I had never explored this area instantly became obvious. Concrete roads and footpaths gradually faded to broken rubble, eventually turning to channels of icy muck. Ahead lay two massive chimneys that belched smoke, the dark, sombre clouds framing grey blocks that diminished in size to houses as we went, finally shrinking to old wooden huts. It was a desolate part of town, poor and decayed-looking, and it was the first time since my arrival that the depth of poverty here hit home to me.

We hopped down one of the frozen, muddy roadways. It must have been a mile or more long, for by the time we got to our destination it was just about dark. An old shed that gasped smoke from a lopsided chimney stood near the roadside. Pigs ran around the garden in a festivity of cold muck and in the shed sat a man dressed in about five coats, mending about fifteen more. There was a particularly noxious smell in the place, possibly emanating from a dog that lay beneath the feet of the man, a dog neither alive nor dead but simply extant, like the furniture. A stove was busy in the corner, the only source of heat, and not much at that, while the rest of the room was lost in shadow.

The man, perhaps in his late seventies, grabbed my coat and stuck his finger through the hole that I had made.

He shook his head a few times and had a look at the buttons, mumbling to himself and smiling. Finally, he agreed to do the job and said to come back in three days' time.

I was told that he was one of the best tailors in town. And when I went back three days later, alone, the job was done. I went to pay him, but not before shaking an old, dirty and very tired hand. All he asked for was about the equivalent of fifty cent.

The question of poverty was, of course, an issue that had been raised several times before our departure to Poland. We had been told to avoid wearing designer labels in the classroom, to choose articles carefully from magazines so they didn't emphasise wealth and to try not to make a fuss about the facilities in the schools, which were sure to be below par.

The facilities in my school were a bit wanting, but the place was spotless and well-run. There was one photocopier, and to get access to it you almost needed a retina scan. At times there would be no paper or no toner, so if a lesson relied on material copied for each student you could be left high and dry. After several aborted lessons due to lack of materials, I decided that sending a couple of kids down to the town to copy whatever I needed was the simplest way. To think, I taught for five years without a text book and had to rely on a dodgy photocopier and self-help books for English teachers.

There were two tape recorders in a locked cupboard in the English room, which I soon discovered were the only two tape recorders in the school. Anyhow, they weren't much use. Anything played above half volume sounded like a swarm of bees behind a newspaper, so again I relied on my own resources and brought my stereo to school.

There was no television at all. After months of contemplating the usefulness of a telly, I eventually started a campaign to get one. The school, however, was broke, and it was two years before a television appeared in the English room. But it was worth it in the end, if only to kill off a dull Monday showing movies.

As time went on, things improved steadily. But even the chalk was hopeless. God knows what it was made of – granite, probably. It didn't write on the blackboard unless the board was wet. So every half an hour I would send a kid out to the bathroom to wet a cloth, which in turn would be used to wet the board. Eventually I found a box of real chalk in a shop and it did the trick.

Aside from the paucity of resources in the school, the fear that we were facing a cultural impasse because of wealth was nonsense. On the very first day, after the opening ceremony, the director and I went to have lunch with the English teachers. The heat had been too much for me, so I went to change out of my sweaty trousers and shirt and into a pair of jeans and a T-shirt. When I came back down, he smiled at me and told the English teacher who was with us that I could wear whatever I wanted in the class. It was good to have a young teacher from the

West in the school, and the kids might learn something, he said. He was right. So long as you didn't show off your wealth – not that I was wealthy anyway – the kids were mature and sensible enough to be aware of modern trends without feeling they would never get to become part of them.

However, there was always a percentage of students in my classes who came from rural communities and who evidently lived in fairly impoverished conditions. There was nothing immediate that told you this, and none of them were in danger of starving. But eventually you would start to notice things. They would shy away from buying new books. Some would use the same copybook for several subjects – the front for maths, the middle for history and the back for English. English was always at the back, which upset me a little. You would soon discover that many had lost fathers, mothers, or both. Yet they were tough, formidable kids, who spoke matter-of-factly when asked about their families, often volunteering information in essays that were read aloud quite freely in class. In the beginning, I was wary about what kind of questions I asked, but seeing that they were open and resilient when it came to sensitive subjects, I became more relaxed also. I enjoyed talking to them. Of course, there were plenty of kids whose folks were doing well, just like in any other society in Europe.

The simple thing to do with the tailor would have been to hand over four or five times the asking price. But to do that would have been to imbalance a whole way of life. Similarly, the temptation was there sometimes in the markets to overpay and congratulate yourself. In some of the markets of Warsaw, or those nearer the borders with Russia, old women sat on pieces of cardboard in the depths of winter, displaying the items from their own homes. It was a pretty wretched sight – photos of their family in meagre frames, cracked cups, rosary beads, socks that didn't match, even objects that would have belonged to those now deceased, like an old pair of glasses. This was the sum total of their wealth and they were prepared to barter with it. You would see them on trains, many coming from the far reaches of the eastern borders with large nylon bags full of rubbish. They might travel a full day, only to sit on a piece of cardboard and sell their few possessions.

There were also people who specialised in the most absurd objects. Down at the market you would find a man who simply sold shoelaces. That was his living. I brought this up in class and made a joke about it. But in Poland, people didn't throw their shoes out just because of a hole or a loose heel. They brought them to a shoemaker, got them repaired and maybe even held onto them until another member of the family could use them. Laces snap more often than a sole wears out, so why shouldn't someone make a living out of them? Sure, hadn't I been desperate to find someone to sew buttons on a coat?

A Man Goes to a Doctor

In the bleak mid-winter, somewhere around early December, I was plotting all kinds of schemes to buy some time off. I was worn out and feeling a bit homesick, and had developed an interesting strain of colour blindness from the snow that wasn't a pure white, but more a shade of grey.

This colour filled my every morning. As I shuffled to school, staring at my feet for treacherous patches of ice, it was a colour that got inside my head and remained there, clouding and dulling the brain. Worse, it was the same colour as the sky most of the time, so even looking up did no good. It was a colour that drove you to bury your head in a bottle or a pillow.

Around this time I had a particularly heavy weekend. It involved a party with some Polish people who had concocted a strange brew that they referred to as 'whiskey'. It wasn't whiskey at all. It was clear for a start, and it was very sweet. I later discovered it was called 'bimber', and was a type of poitín that really packed a punch. It punched and it kicked, and when it was all over it left you sitting in the bathroom whimpering for days afterwards. I prayed for sickness but it didn't come. Few bugs withstand the temperatures here in winter, so illnesses are rare until spring. I couldn't wait until spring.

After the first lesson on the Monday, I inform one of the English teachers that I'm ill. She knows what's wrong. It is simply the vodka hangover that I described earlier. The vodka malaise, the one that imbues the sufferer with such apathy that if the world were coming to an end it would merely be welcomed. When people are perplexed by the laxity in the workplace of former communist states, they clearly have no appreciation of the effect of vodka on the human spirit. And at eight o'clock on a Monday morning, thirty-five screaming girls, no matter how beautiful they are as individuals, make no pretty picture.

I assumed I could just say I was sick, go home and spend a few days in bed. But because I am working for a State institution, my medical health insurance is the same as it would be for a Polish person. To get a sick note I have to go to the local 'polyclinic' to be inspected by a State nurse. If deemed sick enough, I'll then be given a 'zwolnienie', a 'free note', for a week or as long as necessary. So off I go to convince the State.

The polyclinic is a large block with little to distinguish it from its neighbouring blocks but for the red sign on the wall. These signs, which are your staid, functional communist insignias, are placed on all State buildings and institutions, from schools and surgeries to civic offices and even hotels. The typical sign might very bluntly read 'The Primary Music School of the District of Minsk Mazowiecki on Kazikowskiego Street', the sign itself no bigger than a newspaper. Such signs will soon be phased out, of course. But the hilarious thing is that such is their prevalence, people who have opened their own shops or businesses are unable to consider doing much different. Their stores are still named after their function, with the occasional addition of the family name or that of their firstborn child to distinguish it from a State-owned property. You might stumble upon a shoe shop called 'Shoe Shop Agnieszka', or a pub called 'Drink Bar Peter', with those less creative simply calling their vegetable shop 'Vegetables'. At least you know what you're getting and, as the name would suggest, the 'poly' clinic is where a specialist for every part of the body can be found.

As with most public buildings in winter, the inside of the polyclinic is protected from the intense cold by a massive dark curtain, as thick as a carpet, immediately inside its doors. When walking into a dark curtain, it is human nature to bend the head forward, and many people have had to go straight back into the polyclinic having nutted themselves on the way out. If you do make it through in one piece, a wall of stifling, stale heat smacks you in the face.

Upon entering, you go to a hatch to talk to a nurse and explain, briefly, what is wrong with you. Having described your symptoms at the hatch, you present your ID, in my case a teacher's ID, for inspection.

These IDs are gold dust here – you can't even board a

train without one. But to make life a little more tricky, there are a few types. There is the basic ID, which gives your general credentials, from date and place of birth to your current residence, parents' names and so on. Then there is your professional identification, which denotes your status as a student, teacher, civil servant or whatever. These particular IDs entitle you to subsidised travel on trains and buses, as much as fifty percent depending on your occupation – teachers are quite high up in terms of social standing, and are entitled to the full fifty percent. They are one of a few useful documents you have to carry with you.

Finally, there is your medical ID, a sort of logbook that keeps track of all your visits to State clinics, the types of illness you were suffering from at the time and the drugs you were prescribed. It's kept for life and is a handy little document – when you start getting older you can read over your history and get a fair idea of what you're likely to croak from and when. But the number of times I lost my medical ID, and the suffering I had to endure to have it replaced, was worse than any illness that I remember. And I can remember quite a lot about being sick in Poland with or without that book.

I broke a wrist falling after a long night in a pub. I blamed the cobblestones, which were covered in black ice, but the doctors knew better and put a heavy cast on it for my troubles. I put my back out on another occasion and was almost two months out of school. I begged to get back into school, such was the boredom of sitting at home. Once you've been given a sick note by the State clinic, however, you're not allowed out until you've fully recovered or until the period on the 'zwolnienie' has passed. If you're seen rambling around on the streets, there will be problems, questions will be asked, and you could even be docked money. I could never understand that rule, and am convinced it is just some odd quirk that has hung over from the commies. But I stuck to it nonetheless.

Having established the fact that you're sick, you are given a ticket, a room number and a floor level, which should match you up to the right doctor or nurse. If you make a mistake at this point, you could wind up in God knows what department, being probed with God knows what kind of implement in God knows which orifice. So it is vital to get your symptoms right. I have been told by the staff in school to say I have a sore throat, since it is quite likely a teacher will get a sore throat, and a teacher with a sore throat isn't much use and needs time off to recover.

When I find my appointed room, I take a seat on a bench beside a long line of invalids. The old woman next to me has a chest that sounds like a sawmill. At regular intervals, she looks up wide-eyed and bellows at the ceiling. Each cough from her triggers a chain reaction of coughing down along the queue. And maybe it's just me, but there is a menacing sense of the Grim Reaper all around. The place is vacuously bare, with long corridors and hollow, banging doors that bring to mind a morgue. Nobody says anything and everyone looks sicker than they probably are, shivering and moaning, wrapped in bundles and possessed of a far-off gaze like dead sheep.

Like so many waiting areas, this doesn't seem like a good place for the sick. It would either make you sick if you're not already sick, or sicker if you are. However, it is clean and there is a system in place that has already filtered patients without the use of an overpriced GP. Private doctors do exist here, mostly expensive off-duty public doctors working evenings.

At least all these people will be seen and treated by the end of the day, even if it is going to be a long day. They won't be lying on trolleys for weeks, and it's all paid for by the State. If you do go to a private doctor – like I did when my back went out – the chances are they'll tell you to go to the hospital anyway if further treatment is needed.

Hours pass and many sleep like the dead. But a sudden click of the lock on the door and the reaction is like a hare released at a greyhound track. People shout and wave bits of paper, doctors appear and push back the mob while hoarse kids scream at their mothers. In all this chaos, there is nothing I can do but wait until it has calmed down. I go with the flow of the crowd until I'm swept, like a piece of flotsam, onto a cushioned chair in front of a nurse.

The nurse is a friendly, but naturally a suspicious, woman. Heard every hard luck story and is not prepared to give me an easy go of it just because I'm a foreigner. A hangover would instil little sympathy, and I have been warned not to mention my numb right foot, so I have to try something else. Here I am passed my wild card. She hands me a thermometer and sends me outside. I am to sit with it under my armpit while the next patient is dealt with. Realising my thermometer is not going to reach the stars, I go into the bathroom and run it under the hot tap until it hits a sufficiently frightful level. Temperature levels panic Polish nurses in winter, so she gives me a list of drugs and a week off. Miraculously, she actually discovers a sore throat I didn't know I had, so it has all worked out very well in the end.

With a week off, I line up a few books I've been meaning to read and settle into bed to relax. I feel good now. The snow is pelting the windows and I can hear the rushed footsteps of the kids outside as they dash from boarding block to school. I'm in such a childishly joyous mood, in fact, that I even look at my watch every hour and figure out what class I'm missing, what tripe will be served up for dinner and what temperature it'll be come dusk. At lunchtime, some of the kids arrive with a tray of soup and bread, a few cartons of juice and some chocolate. They wish me a speedy recovery, and I'm very moved at that. I thank them, but tell them that I've no intention of speeding up the recovery. The day passes nice and slowly, most of it spent reading and sleeping, with no further plans but for more of the same the next day.

The next morning at precisely eight o'clock, however, a cruel intervention takes place. In the middle of a nice doze there comes a deafening, ear-splitting noise and immediately a bit from a pneumatic drill pierces the wall, missing my ear by only a few inches. I leap off the bed and stare in disbelief at the wall beside my pillow. The bit is gone, but the evidence, a white powdery circle of chewed up plaster, lies lifeless on my sheet. Just then, there is a knock on my door and almost simultaneously the bulbs blink out all over my flat like dodgy Christmas lights.

I open the door, my face frozen in fear, as much through the implications of that drill as the near miss. It is the director of the boarding school, who tells me the corridor is going to be rewired and the power will be off during the day for the next couple of weeks. Because of the inconvenience of moving me out, they have decided my flat will be left alone. Everyone else, however, will be moved to another wing. The door closes. The drill kicks into life again next door. No lights for reading, no stereo for music, nothing to do and a whole week to do it in.

For the week, I bathe in candlelight and spend my time daydreaming. I'm now forced to eat the boarding school food because there's no power and I can't get to the shops or cafés. The workers traipse in and out of my flat all day, because the main fuse box is located in the hallway. That doesn't really bother me; I just stay in the main room. Each evening when they finish – any time between six and ten – I remind them to turn the power back on for my section. Then the problems really start.

Every evening when power is restored, they have managed to mess something else up. After they are gone, I might discover that the kitchen light works, but the main room is left in darkness. Or a socket on one side is operable and the rest dead. Whenever I enquire, they simply tell me that everything will be fine eventually, and not to worry. The word 'eventually', similarly used by Marx, Lenin and the rest of the boys, has scary connotations in Poland.

Despite the inconvenience, I am glad that the power problem is finally being looked at. It was a complete mess. There were nights when the fuse box in the hall hummed and droned like a bumble bee – it was only a matter of time before it either exploded or burned the building down while we all slept peacefully in our beds. But about three weeks later, when the boys were just about to pack up, the bathroom light suddenly died.

In they came, two of them. The first went into the bathroom and played with the switch a few times while prodding the suspended bulb with the end of his cigarette. Then he went out and looked at the new fuse box, pulling at his bottom lip and muttering something not very promising under his breath. The pair then had a sort of discussion and finally turned to me. 'Nie bylo,' they said.

This means literally, 'it wasn't there', and is far graver than 'nie ma', 'it's not there', which at least implies some hope. In other words, they were saying that there never was a light in the bathroom. Then they walked out. That was it. I was left standing in the bathroom staring at a light that never existed, trying to figure out a way to get round the problem. George Orwell had given a name to this approach in his alarmingly familiar *1984* – he called it 'doublethink'.

The process of doublethink was used by the Party in Orwell's tale to cover up any mistakes that had been made, and involved simply negating a matter in your mind and replacing it with whatever the Party told you to. It took a bit of practice, but appeared to work – at least for the Party. Applying the process of doublethink to my situation was simple. They had made a mistake when installing the new fuse box and clearly forgot to connect up the bathroom light. It was a mistake they didn't want to remedy – the wiring was finished and that was the end of it.

That evening, the director of the school and the school electrician were called over after I mentioned it to the director of the internat. He also looked at it, prodded it with his cigarette and, after a discussion that was mostly made up of shrugs, turned to me and asked if I was sure I'd really had a light.

What do you do in a situation like that? I said, okay, let's imagine there never was a light there. Now, is there a possibility of getting a new light? There was a pregnant pause as both studied the fixture. Finally, the electrician gave a more reassuring shrug.

It was left to another electrician, who arrived a few mornings later with a pair of eyes that looked as if they'd been roasted over a grill. He shuffled about the flat flicking switches and cursing until I gave him a beer from the fridge. He smiled, clapped me on the back and said it would be finished by the time I got back from school. True to his word, the light was fixed by the time I got back. All the beer and a full bottle of flavoured vodka were also gone from the fridge. This wasn't stealing though. He considered it to be his bribe or 'gift', since bribes were rarely in the form of money, but more often chocolate, coffee or vodka. If I had done likewise with the first bunch of guys, the light might very well have existed all along. You live and learn.

So Happy Christmas,
I Love You Baby

It's Christmas in Poland and all through the house, not a
creature was drinking, not even a mouse. A little amend-
ment to the traditional rhyme that went through my head
after spending my first Christmas away from home. I
didn't go home the first year, because I wanted to see
what it was like here at Christmas. I had another reason
also, which I'll get into shortly.

I had heard all about the Polish Christmas from the kids
in school, who seemed to love the idea so much you'd
swear they still believed in Santa Claus. But any lingering
doubts about the existence of Santa Claus were truly shattered on the streets of Warsaw on a bitterly cold afternoon
three days before Christmas Eve. Off one of the main thor-
oughfares, a twisted drunk Santa stumbled past me, beard
hanging off one ear and a pair of eyes like two glowing
coals receding into the back of his red hood. He was singing a Polish hymn and in his hand was a bottle of Spiritus.

Spiritus is the staple for winos, a lethal, pure alcoholic
concoction that would fuel a combine harvester. For the
benefit of those who can't read, there's a graphic on the

front – something like a skull and crossbones. At least it's better than the cherry wine that other diehards drink here. That has a picture of a naked woman on the label and costs the equivalent of about fifty cent. Lord knows what supermarket this Santa had been working in, but he had probably ruined Christmas for hundreds of kids before eventually being turfed out onto the streets to sing his hymns.

That jolly wino was an exception to the rule in a country where traditions are still upheld rigorously, the banning of alcohol featuring regularly. The Polish people simply shrug and accept it, used to the intervention of the Church in affairs of the State. Advent and Lent are periods when it is forbidden to 'party', while alcohol is banned completely over Christmas until after St Stephen's Day.

In fact, such is the paranoia over alcohol, that beer advertising was eventually banned. However, some clever breweries found a way around this, by manufacturing alcohol-free beer. Suddenly, loads of useless beer began to appear on the shelves. The fact that the 'new' beer was alcohol-free was very subtly expressed, the small, 33cl bottles lavishly packaged in a six-pack and the lack of alcohol evident only by careful study of the small print on the label.

For a country where alcohol-free beer was not only a new innovation, but a contradiction in terms, it never occurred to people to study the labels. Even the television ads were understated, with a brief two-word statement whispered at the end of an ad – featuring some young girl swooning over a man with a bottle – to say it was 'without alcohol'. With the difference in packaging between the real product and the alcohol-free one insignificant, they were still advertising 'beer' as far as we were concerned.

The local booze-hounds, myself included, all bought the 'new' beer, of course. It featured a new innovation for Polish society – bottles that you didn't have to bring back. Now that was progress, something definitely worth celebrating.

Depending on how you looked at it, the fact that empty bottles were usually indispensable was either a Godsend or a curse. To buy a half-dozen beers in the store you needed to have a half-dozen empties with you or you were charged a lot more. By the same token, returning a half-dozen empties meant a few bob on their own. Bottles were good business, and were treated as such. For winos, most of the day was spent trawling through bushes and along the sides of railway tracks, where careless folk or other winos had mistakenly discarded their bottles. A good day's pickings could yield several free beers or a few sausages, depending on which you craved more at the time.

For people like myself, forced to maintain an air of decency when heading to the shops for beer, having to leave the internat with a bag of empty bottles clanging together like bells was an embarrassing and cumbersome experience. But you couldn't throw empty bottles in the bin, and you didn't want a stockpile mounting up under the sink. It all changed one night when I thought I had devised a noiseless way of getting empty bottles out and full ones back in.

The suede coat I had by now grown accustomed to was a monstrosity to look at, but a blessing indeed for its soundproofing. There was no way the human ear could detect the clink of bottles under that coat. On a Friday night, when no trips into the pale of Warsaw had been arranged, off I'd go to the store with three or four bottles down the front of my trousers and one in each of the pockets, the coat providing adequate cover all the while.

One night, however, I was in my pyjamas, but feeling rather restless. It was a Thursday, one of those evenings where you weren't tired but you didn't really feel like doing very much either. So I pulled on a pair of jeans and shoved a few empty bottles down the front. Leaving the pyjama top on, I threw the suede coat over the whole lot and headed off to buy a few beers.

I was only a few yards down the road when I bumped into my director. He had had a few drinks himself, and was delighted to see me. So delighted, in fact, that he decided we should celebrate and invited me to the local café. I shook my head as vigorously as I could, explaining that I had left the lights on. He waved his hand and began pulling me by the sleeves. I continued that I had left the electric heater on also, figuring that would cause more of a reaction. No, not a thing. As if things weren't bad enough, he elected that the café wasn't a good idea after all, and that we'd go to one of the English teachers' houses instead. There was no going back.

To make things worse, I had been trying to seduce the daughter of this English teacher. It was a ridiculous idea, really. Her mother had been constantly talking about her in the staff room – how her boyfriend was a doctor, how she was studying law and also getting her advanced diploma in piano, how she worked part-time as a music teacher and so on. Eventually, I felt I had to meet her and awaited an opportunity.

One Sunday evening I was invited to dinner. I was already teaching the younger daughter, so I knew two out of the four members of the family. I did my best to look presentable, brought the wine, flowers and chocolates, but I had been away for the weekend with the Irish gang and wasn't in great shape. I took off my shoes, as was customary, and realised I had holes in my socks. And I think I attacked the roast chicken with the vigour of a man starved for weeks, which wasn't far from the truth. The worst thing that happened, however, was that I fell instantly, head over heels, for her daughter, Asha, from the first handshake.

I knew it was going to happen at some stage. The Polish girls had been gradually wrecking my head. They have a particular beauty and a manner that is infectious. They are tough and direct, but also ridiculously romantic, to the point of being almost naïve. I found Polish girls to be possessed of a magnetism that would draw you in and leave you helpless.

I had to stand in front of hundreds of them every day, and most of them weren't much younger than myself. That in itself was a cruelty, and I knew that it was only a matter of time before one of them blew me away. That it had to be a teacher's daughter was particularly unfair. Here I was, a blow-in on a year's contract, who had infiltrated their school as a pseudo-teacher and had no clue as to what the future might hold. There was she, the daughter of a teacher in my school, going out with a doctor and on her way to becoming a lawyer. It really made no sense. Pursuing it was entirely unethical. But bollocks to that.

My decision was mulled over with some of the Irish guys, who made it plain that if I started seeing this girl, I was in for the long haul. Poles seemed serious about relationships, and marriage came early. Girls in school were constantly telling me that they were going to marry their present boyfriends. These were eighteen-year-olds, with their lives ahead of them. I begged them not to, of course. But there seemed to be no stopping them.

The idea of marriage terrified me, though. I left home to pursue wanton hedonism and independence, not to get married, no sir. If I embarked on a relationship with a Polish girl whose mother I had to face in the staff room each morning, then there could only be one destination – the altar of a Polish church.

So, on this evening, only my second or third time to meet Asha, I removed my shoes and coat to reveal four empty beer bottles stuck down the front of my jeans, barely hidden by my pyjamas. The two in the pockets I had managed to lash into the snow en route when the director wasn't looking. From now on, I decided, the empties would remain under the sink until I was able, on a monthly basis and under cover of darkness, to deposit them in the bushes for the winos.

And so it came to pass, at Christmas time, that these new bottles heralded in a whole new way of shopping for booze. Or so we thought. Soon there were riots in the stores, as people protested at having spent a fortune on the fancy new six-packs without even getting a buzz. For the breweries it was a victory. They got their brand on the television and in the magazines regardless.

Eventually, in 2001, the ban was amended – adverts were permitted on radio, television and in cinemas between the hours of 11pm and 6am, but prohibited from videos, youth-oriented magazines, front pages of all magazines and billboards. Also, no ad, regardless of where it appeared, could now feature imagery where the beer in question was somehow associated with 'sexual attractiveness', 'free time' or 'health'. Only in Poland.

These rather draconian measures imposed by Church and State could have been averted had the PPPPs come to power. The *Polska Partia Przyjaciol Piwa* – literally translated as the Polish Party for Friends of Beer, but more commonly referred to as the Beer Lover's Party – began its political life as a bit of a joke, but soon developed into a party of some standing, albeit short-lived.

Formed in December 1990, the PPPP's manifesto concentrated on freedom of association and expression, intellectual tolerance and a higher standard of living. The beer part entered into the equation since they also wished to promote lively discussion in good pubs with good beer. Their humorous name helped them win votes from a rather disillusioned populace in the 1991 parliamentary elections – they gained an amazing total of sixteen *Sejm* (Senate) seats. However, following a split within the PPPP in 1992 into the Big Beer Party and the Little Beer Party – Polish politics has more splits than a team of gymnasts – the former lost their sense of humour and became the Polish Economic Program, forming a coalition with myriad other parties that I won't even begin to get into. Again, only in Poland.

To be fair, a lot of people don't bother abstaining at Christmas. But in smaller rural towns, you don't have much of a choice. Shops and bars, where they exist, close up well before Christmas Eve and the place becomes a ghost town. If you do manage to find a store open on or just before Christmas Eve, you'll discover that the shelves have been emptied. It stays that way until well into the new year, all the shops remaining closed for 'stock--taking'. Stock-taking, when there's actually no stock, is a mystery. More mysterious still is the fact that it takes a full week to count this no stock. So, to survive, you have to harvest as much food as you can to get you through Christmas and into the new year.

I wasn't prepared for any of this the first year and went wombling around the streets just before Christmas Eve, foraging in vain for a bit of jar and some food. The results of my search were too depressing to describe, but I was kindly invited to the home of my saviour, the English teacher, for Christmas – an invitation I accepted gratefully, as otherwise I would have been found dead in mid-January, clinging to the door of an empty fridge.

I also saw this as a good opportunity to get presents in ahead of the doctor in Warsaw. I had, by this stage, the few 'dates' to my credit and figured a good spell over the Christmas would do the trick.

The dating game was all very old-fashioned. It kind of reminded me of tales of my parents, how they first met up and what they did on dates – sharing a single of chips, sitting and watching the river flow by, that sort of thing. In the background, of course, always lurked the mother, rather unfairly represented as the ogre figure that had to be dodged, bribed or softened up at all times.

Each date necessitated a flower for the girl and chocolates for the mum. If you wished to go out again, you always met the mother before you took the girl out and after you brought her back if possible. There was a terrible sense of Big Brother on each occasion, particularly when we returned to the flat at the respectable hour of about 10pm. The blocks were all fitted out with prehistoric intercom systems, with a phone inside each flat and a large speaker on the wall next to the door on the outside.

This speaker droned and hummed constantly. There was always a suspicion that people inside the block had picked up the phone and were listening in on the Irishman and the Polish girl standing under the porch in the cold, trying to sneak in a snog before going to say goodnight to the mother.

Buying flowers was another new experience for me. A single man buying a single rose can only mean one thing in Poland – that he has a 'date'. It is very common to see guys – many dressed in suits for the simple evening ahead – walking down the street with a flower early on a Friday evening. You always had to buy flowers in odd numbers. Even numbers are bad luck, which meant you got one or three – usually just the one. Later on the Friday night you'd see the same guys, only with a girl to accompany the flower. Cafés were full of couples on the weekends, each with a flower, and there were flower shops all over town that made a killing selling single roses.

Romance was very much alive and well in Poland, but it wasn't something I was used to. Any experience I had had up to that point at home usually involved meeting a girl at a party or pub and fumbling somewhere in the corner of the room, the back of your ma's car or a convenient public location. If things went smoothly you might see them again at a house party. And, apart from a couple of serious relationships that ran their course when I was growing up or in college, romance was never really there, even if there was a love of sorts. Taking things slowly certainly wasn't part of it. Slow walks, hand-in-hand, and a short parting kiss was never part of it. But in a Polish town, that's what weekends were about.

The Irish guy walking down the street with his single rose was a great laugh for the students, of course. The thing was about two feet long. I tried to hide it under my coat, but the thorns got me. Tongues wagged after the first time, and some of the kids were even brazen enough to ask me in the class.

'Tom, are you having dates with a Polish girl?'

Silence descends on the class. They all stare at me.

'Yes, I am.'

'Ooooh,' they go in unison. 'Who is it?'

'You don't know her.'

'Is she pretty?'

'Yes, and I'm going through something of a crisis.'

In time they found out. There were very few places you could take a girl in the town. You could go to the cinema on a Sunday night and sit with half of your students. You could go to the café and sit with half the students. Or you could walk in the park – with half your students.

If you took a girl to your flat, you may as well have branded her a witch. Strictly forbidden, it was a rule we ignored at times, which meant Asha got a roasting and I got the silent treatment in the staff room. A single girl visiting a single man in his home could only mean that he was a man of bad character, and that she was a brazen hussy. Let the pair of them be damned. If Asha came over, she'd dash into the building with her hat down over her face. If the doors were locked, she'd lob a stone at the window and I'd throw down the keys.

Getting back out was tricky too – we had to break into a sprint past the office, past the prying eyes of whoever was on duty. Sometimes it was a young teacher, Bozena, who would smile and wave, or the PE teacher, Tadek, a great character, who would also just give a short wave. At times we weren't so lucky, though, and the word would be on the street by dawn.

It was frustrating, but I didn't care. I would have gone neck-high through the sewers of the town at the time, because I was star struck. I saw this all as part of the great plan that was written for me.

I turned up most days at the music school where Asha worked as a piano teacher. I would nod politely to the woman who manned the doors and she would allow me to wait in the hall for Miss Zimnicka – I had to use the 'miss' – to finish work so I could escort her home. I would even go to the train station on the nights she attended college, without ever knowing which train she was on. One came in every half-hour, so I'd wander up, have a look, and if she wasn't on it I'd wander home and wait for the next one. It could be eleven o'clock before she'd come in. I'd walk her home to her door, check that the speaker wasn't humming, give her a peck on the cheek and trundle off through the snow to my flat. There was a glimpse through the window in the hallway of her block, and I would stare out into the night sky, a hopeless romantic.

Christmas Eve is when Polish people have their main meal. The Christmas dinner is served up literally when the first star appears. So you have to starve until it gets dark, basically. Depending on your culinary tastes, you would either love or hate the Christmas meal – beetroot or mushroom soup; 'pierogi', little flour pouches stuffed with forest mushrooms and cabbage, which are excellent; cabbage stew; fruit 'kompot'; various salads; those raw herrings again, this time without the vodka; and the pièce de résistance – carp, a muddy little bastard that lives at the bottoms of ponds.

This poor creature suffers a particularly cruel fate. He is kept alive in a bucket of water right up to the moment he's about to land on the grill, whereupon he is ceremoniously battered with a hammer. I couldn't eat much of it after witnessing that, the frozen blood on the balcony visible the whole way through the meal. Anyway, carp has more bones than a graveyard and a texture like the sole of a Doc Martin boot. Instead, I devoured as many of those pierogi things as I could, hoping a magic mushroom may have found its way inside.

Midnight saw the whole town converge on the church for a mass that even the great man himself would be at pains to endure. Lengthy sermons and fire and brimstone were the order of the day as heads bowed and breasts were struck. However, when the sermon steamed into its fortieth minute, a peasant woman at the front stood up and began roaring at the priest. Nobody could explain to me what the outburst was about, but it shocked the priest into getting on with it. By 1.45, we were back on the streets, which glittered in temperatures of −18°C. I could have murdered a pint and a hot whiskey.

That's possibly a harsh picture, maybe even unjust. And to be very honest, there is more of a benign atmosphere here at Christmas than you might find elsewhere. It is far more radiant visually because of the snow, but you also feel that the true meaning of Christmas is fully evident and, whether you're a Christian or not, you can't help but feel that the mood is spiritual.

The streets, even the main road east that's otherwise constantly rumbling with traffic, are deathly still, and the only sounds you're likely to hear are church bells. It is a time for family most of all and the Polish people, who are very into their family gatherings, adore the whole occasion. At the main meal they bless each other and grant each other wishes. They sit around together and sing. Everybody helps to make the dinner, which takes hours, and the house is scrubbed from top to bottom.

Spending Christmas with a family I hadn't known previously was very moving. I was, after all, a stranger, yet I was treated as one of their own. A few of the other Irish teachers who had also been invited to the homes of Polish families that year recounted similar feelings. They felt like intruders, but were treated like brothers.

After those few days, it was obvious to Asha's family what was going on between us. Not that it was easy. The phone rang on Christmas Eve and the boyfriend was on the line. Though my Polish was minimal at the time, I could tell who it was. It was an awkward moment in a place where relationships are taken very seriously. I could have been turfed out in the snow. But I wasn't.

As time went on and things grew more serious between myself and Asha, I was a guest almost every evening in their household. Imagine what it must have been like for a family to have a foreign guest over almost every evening for supper. It was never a conscious decision on my part – I would simply pop over to visit, or would be escorting Asha back from work, and would be asked to stay. It showed the nature of hospitality in Poland, done without any fuss and each time with the same degree of warmth. And for the five years I was there, that never changed.

However, on the down side, it has to be said that Christmas in Poland can get boring without the gargle. Aside from the gin-sodden Santa in Warsaw, you would be unlikely to hear the sound of a boozed-up human on the street until New Year's Eve, when the whole town, as if under water for the week, rises to the surface for a bloody big gulp. Then anything goes. Parties ensue that make the ones back home look very tame. So there is a bit of an anomaly there, unusual for such a Christian country. You sort of do your penance before you head down the sinning route. I suppose it amounts to the same thing in the end.

The day after Christmas Day, Stephen's Day, my eyes light up when I hear we're going over to the local hop in the Palace that lies in the centre of the park. Alas, I'm soon informed that it is a minerals-only affair. My mind descends into a state of dread. Students, hundreds of them, will be there. Being dragged up to dance sober is, well, a sobering affair at the best of times, but being the village idiot in a foreign country goes beyond humiliation.

With the excuse of changing clothes, I rush home and search the flat for anything that might induce a buzz. Finding only a half bottle of cheap wine and some cough syrup, I lash them both back in a rather unhealthy but surprisingly effective cocktail. If I became the village idiot thereafter, at least I did it in style. In fact, I was Lord of the Dance.

The last time I visited Poland for Christmas I bought myself a twenty-four pack of Guinness and a pint glass at the airport and sat guzzling the cans on my own. The family were a bit disgusted at this terrible display of barbarity, but hey, I'm not the one battering a poor carp to death with a hammer on Christmas Eve.

Shelter from the Storm

There is a place over in the northeastern part of Poland called Grabarka, located not far from the border with Bielorussia. Few people travel to the east of Poland unless they have a specific purpose. Nobody travels to Bielorussia. Ever. I asked about it a few times, enquiring why the Poles never went and whether it was worth visiting. The look of astonishment I received was enough to deter me. There is nothing there to see, I was told. Absolutely nothing.

The towns on this side of Poland are more influenced by Russia, and some are tragic, crumbling reminders of the War and the subsequent occupation, their factories and sprawling rail tracks sitting alongside the shells of once beautiful buildings. You might pop into a train station, a cheerless, grey block, and inside it find old features like a carved bench or a large tiled stove, hints that Poland had its glory days. It is a real shame, and for the people of Poland, it must be simply unforgivable.

Most smaller towns in the east are hard to get to by public transport and, even if you do manage to reach your destination, you'll soon realise that there's nothing to keep you there. However, there are some sights worth seeing in these out-of-the-way places. Chopin's home, for example, is located in some oddball town on some labyrinthine route out of Warsaw. I aborted two attempts to get there and, after five years, never got to see it at all.

This part of the country is just not ready to deal with visitors. They don't have the infrastructure, they don't have the budget and perhaps they haven't even considered the economic advantages of tourism. Instead, the region relies on basic trade with the Russians for its few bob, and vice versa. Eventually, it will change. But in the meantime, you need the dedication of a pilgrim on his way to Mecca to complete a journey on this side of the world.

Grabarka, the 'holy mountain', is one of these oddball but well-known sights, located in the middle of nowhere. At least, I thought it was well known, but the truth is that few Polish people seemed aware of its existence. It is a place of worship for the Orthodox community of Poland, who have been coming here on pilgrimages annually since 1710. In that year, a cholera epidemic broke out in the region and decimated the population, the majority of whom were Orthodox. But amidst the despair, a sign of some sort was seen from the mountain and those that reached the top were saved. The mountain thereafter became a place of great sanctity and, as a mark of gratitude, people planted crosses on the top, a tradition which has lasted to this day. The mountain and surrounding forest now contain up to 20,000 crosses. They vary in size, depending on the gravity of the cross planter's sins. I decided to see this place for myself.

'Transport is basically by train, the Sycze station being a short walk from the hill. Trains run regularly from/to Siedlce (63km) and semi-regularly from/to Hajnowka (58km). Only one or two buses link Grabarka to Siemiatycze (9km) and it's better not to rely on them at the time of the festival.'

That's what it says in my Lonely Planet guide. After travelling in this region for some time you learn that such wording is about as close as you can get to the truth. At a bus stop, for example, there will be a timetable with the various times of buses. Beside each time, however, there will be a symbol of some sort – an 'X', a cross, a dollar sign, a number, whatever. Beneath the times there will be a key to each symbol. However, you could have three or four symbols beside one bus, and I am not joking when I say that there could be up to thirty different symbols to decipher altogether. What is really baffling is how the powers-that-be compile the things. You could have a bus that runs on weekdays, not on Saturdays, and only on the first Sunday of every month. You could have a bus that runs only on Tuesdays. You could have a bus that runs on Sundays, unless that Sunday is Easter Sunday. You could have buses that run in winter only, where winter begins on such a date and ends on such a date. At least all of this makes the timetable so large that it is not hard to find a bus stop.

To make things worse, for a bit of a laugh, kids tear off the key to the symbols. If that's gone and you're in unfamiliar territory, start saying your prayers. It happened to me one evening – the bus I was on began drifting in the wrong direction and I ended up in a hamlet lit by one solitary streetlight and containing one bus stop. Not a shop, bar or phone box was to be seen anywhere. It was the middle of winter, it was getting very late and I honestly thought I'd be found dead the following spring. Thankfully, after almost two hours of waiting in freezing temperatures, a bus came the other way. But during those two hours, not one other person did I see. When you are stranded in such a place, you are truly stranded.

To put you in the picture, Minsk, my town, lies about forty kilometres east of Warsaw. Forty kilometres further east, you come to the capital of the region of Mazowiecki, a town that takes two years of work to pronounce: Siedlce. This town, with a population about twice the size of Minsk, doesn't have an entry in the Lonely Planet either. Considering it is the capital of the region, that doesn't bode well. The reason why lands on you like cold water as soon as you rattle into the place on one of the old iron monsters that serve the local stations here.

There are two types of train in Poland, the first being the Intercity trains which have first-class, second-class and express services. Clean, comfortable and reliable, these serve the major cities nationwide and are a joy to travel on. The second type is the 'osobisty', a local beast that rumbles along like a cattle cart. A faded orange colour on the outside, with hard, plastic seats on the inside, this machine stops ruggedly at every outpost along the way. This may be merely a platform, with nothing to give away the fact that it's a station save perhaps an old woman huddled on a broken bench. A stretch on one of these rattlers is an experience that can turn the most enthusiastic mind into a dullard. At first sight, most would make the decision not to get on at all. This would probably be a wise move – after dark, at least – since crime is rife on these things.

Pulling in to Siedlce, the only way you know you've arrived somewhere more than a mere platform is by the quantity of tracks jutting in all directions, like the guts of some iron dinosaur torn apart with a claw hammer. Platforms are dark, decaying, concrete slabs that look rusted, if that's possible. They are littered with motionless people, the collars of their coats up around their faces no matter what time of year. Beggars, cripples, limping dogs – poverty hangs in the air like a ghost. The station café is a bit rough, with a large congregation of homeless people, but a glass of their bullet-proof coffee does the job.

The waiting room is no better and the town nondescript, save for a large prison on the main street, so I head quickly to get a ticket to that place called Szycze, sixty-three kilometres away.

The woman at the ticket hatch has never heard of it, and she doesn't have a map. Neither has the information point. Anyway, it doesn't matter, I'm told that I won't be going to wherever Szycze is, since it's most likely on the northeast line and I need to get to Hajnowka first, and that train is gone. It is that simple. So I have to go into the town to find the bus station.

The bus station in Siedlce, about ten minutes' walk from the train station, consists of a small, decaying, one-room building and a line of iron barriers outside for the buses. Checking the timetable, I discover that whoever compiled it flew right past the logic department again. All the buses to where I want to go leave at exactly the same times as the trains. Absurd, pure and simple. I resolve to head for a place called Biala Podlaska, where one of my Irish colleagues lives. If I can't make it to Hajnowka today, at least I'll have a place to stay tonight.

An hour later, the bus to Biala arrives on a thick blanket of fumes, pulling up at one of the iron barriers. A feature-less driver snaps the tickets out of people's hands and we all shudder as the engine kicks in. Once out of Siedlce, though, that tightness that grips your chest relaxes as the countryside opens up. It is a welcome sight. Poland is quite flat and, in keeping with the country's name, derived from the word 'pola', meaning 'field', most of what you see driving through it are precisely fields.

They look vast, peaceful and soothing. They are lonely though, and empty too, save the odd farmer sweeping through them with a scythe, or a cow chained to a stick near a ditch. Many of the fields dip in the centre from stag-nant pools formed after heavy spring rain and poor drainage – farmers certainly have their work cut out here with monotonous flooding. Poland needs a better infrastructure badly and the farmers need a hand out. Somehow, though, I get the feeling that it won't happen for a while. There are just too many of them with very little to offer, God bless them. I reckon they'll be swallowed up.

The few pigs and cows they have get them very little at the market, so they keep their grandparents at home instead. 'It pays more for a farmer to keep his grandparents than four cows. Grandparents don't give milk, but they have regular pensions,' one of the farmers from the Self Defence Farmer's Union said about the situation in rural Poland. People have wondered why nursing homes are a rarity in this country; now they have the answer.

Like the trains, buses tend to differ in quality. Private coach companies have been moving in from abroad, setting up long-distance operations between the major cities. This fills a gaping hole in the market, but at the cost of the public service, which has no funds to improve itself.

The public buses vary in much the same way as items in a second-hand clothes shop. Old, out-of-date and smelling of wee, they do the job but not with any great elegance. It is amazing how unhygienic a bus seat can be, after about fifty years of peasants' bums.

The very worst thing about the buses, however, is the music. Unlike most public transport systems, in which a driver might travel different routes and on different buses, Polish drivers usually have the one bus for the duration of their careers. They tend to customise it according to their tastes, with stickers, pendants, crosses, pictures of Jesus and the Pope and, of course, their own stereo and music collection. In the majority of cases, the music is a brand known as 'Disco Polo', a poorly produced imitation of nineties continental disco with a hint of Polish folk thrown in. The result is unsettling.

Disco Polo is heard in virtually every café, shop, bar and restaurant, particularly in eastern Poland and particularly in the countryside. Even a glance at the names of some of the groups is enough to have a red flag waved: Boys, Shazza, Max and Mario, Cassanova and so on. Cheap videos shot at cold, windy beaches on the Baltic; tacky songs such as 'Sex on the Beach (come on everybody)', 'Revolution in Paradise' and 'Tarzan Boy' – *'Tarzan handsome, Tarzan strong, from the jungle, love me long. Tarzan handsome, Tarzan strong, he looks cute and his hair is long.'*

There are a great many talented musicians in this country, but there are few jobs. What jobs there are don't pay. People who play in the army bands or orchestras might have a solid job. But if you live in a village and your dream is to head to the big smoke to get a recording deal or get into a jazz scene, you have a tough road ahead. What do you do? You turn to this Disco Polo, because it will guarantee a good income. Sadly and inexplicably, it has a huge market. This worries me greatly, and should really worry the Poles. The buses of course, act as seed carriers, spreading it throughout the country and beyond. And while the Polish people themselves are very welcome in Ireland, let us pray that none of these buses are allowed to cross our borders.

The following week, on Saturday, at seven o'clock in the morning, I'm ready for my second attempt to find Grabarka. I've done my homework, and have times of the various trains worked out. The only problem is that I don't know how to get back and, with the mention of 'semi--regular' trains in the guidebook for the return leg, I'm not very confident either. For some reason, the warm spring weather we had been enjoying until recently has been transformed into an ill-fated spate of hail, battered dark skies and a razor for a wind.

Siedlce again, looking even worse in the rain. An hour to kill in the station, then the train out to Grabarka. One of the more disturbing aspects of local train travel in these remote areas is that most of the stations are unmarked. In fact, they're not stations at all, just platforms which interrupt an otherwise unbroken spread of fields and wood. If you're on a line for the first time, you have to count the stops and it would be madness to travel at night if you didn't know where you were going.

At Grabarka station (a bare platform) I get off, noticing that I'm the only one doing so. This is a bad sign. As the train disappears, not a sinner is to be seen and the lonely clank of a cowbell is the only sound to be heard through the wind.

I'm looking for a mountain. But there's only hilly forest on either side of the track, separated by a large clearing of fields on the right. The fields are dotted with wooden houses and the area is split in two by a narrow country road. The sky overhead is like a two-tone slab of marble, white and grey, spilling a shower of rice-grain-sized hail that stings. As I move quickly towards the thick pine forest on my left for shelter, there's a nasty voice telling me that not only am I not going to find this mountain, but I'm not going to find a way home either. There is no bus stop, no station, and no timetable anywhere.

A half-hour later, I'm trudging through the forest on the left of the track without having met a soul. Stopping to pee up against a tree, I consider just trying to go home and warning people that travel to this place is not to be recommended. I hate giving up though. I'm standing on a slight rise now and stare across at the other side of the track. The sun has come out a little, and I convince myself to explore that part before throwing in the towel.

Crossing the track, I stroll down the hill to where a few wooden houses stand. In the yard of the first house, a man is chopping wood. A few chickens tear around aimlessly, and an old peasant woman stands watching at the gate. She has her hair wrapped up in a bundle under a large red scarf, and her body in an assortment of other various-coloured clothing. Her arms fold across two giants of busts as she leans down on the gate and waits for me to come closer.

I go over to ask her where the hell Grabarka is supposed to be.

'Is it Grabarka or the Holy Mountain you're looking for?'

'The Holy Mountain, I think.'

'It's not a Catholic place, you know,' she says, squinting one eye.

Since Poland is ninety-four percent Catholic, such responses are normal. Although, to be honest, any flame of an urge to practise my Catholic faith was well smothered after only a year here. When I was living at home, I went to mass on a Sunday. It was a habit as much as anything else, a ritual that somehow fulfilled a desire for inner peace once a week. Half the time, I would stand in the porch daydreaming, but the mass was short and the sermon had a semblance of a point, and there was nothing very arduous about it.

Jesus himself wouldn't stick mass in Poland, and I left one Sunday so utterly dejected and dispirited that I knew I simply couldn't go again. Old women caw up at the crosses with mouths wide open and eyes dilated, their bead-wrapped knuckles quivering in prayer. The priest, meanwhile, pummels the podium, screaming and shouting at his clergy who all stand frozen like statues. Religion is supposed to lift the soul, not smother it.

Of course, religious fervour here has its roots. During the Russian occupation, the leader of the Polish church, Cardinal Wyszinski, a determined and strong-willed man, acted as a direct conduit from the Polish people to the Vatican. The people's voice from behind the iron curtain substantially came through him. With the appointment of John Paul II as Pope and his pilgrimage in 1979, the spirit of the people was greatly lifted – it was this visit that undoubtedly influenced the Solidarity movement. In recent history at least, Poland owes a large debt to the Church. But the Church has a worrying hold over the people, which doesn't always seem healthy.

So when this countrywoman told me it wasn't a Catholic place, it was said on the presumption that I was.

When I tell her I am simply here to see it as a tourist, she goes out of her way to give directions, confusingly providing me with three routes of varying lengths. She must have noticed my confusion, because twenty minutes later into the woods a young guy on a bike comes up behind me.

'I am here to show you the mountain,' he says to me.

'No, I'm okay,' I tell this guy, 'I'll manage.'

'But my mother sent me, and you are to come back for tea afterwards.'

Again I decline. I'm not in the mood for too much talking; I really just want to ramble around on my own. The young guy insists though, so finally I give in and follow him through the woods to the mountain.

The 'mountain' turns out to be a small and disappointing hill. It must have been pretty crowded up there during the cholera outbreak. Piotr, my new guide, takes me first to a well at the bottom, with a small, whitewashed wall around it and a blue roof over it. A clear stream trickles into the well from the woods and apparently people with assorted skin diseases come here all the time to bathe their feet in the waters. As Piotr reaches into the well with one of the receptacles hanging beside it, the image of three hundred years of feet fills my mind.

'You have to drink it,' he says. 'That's why people come here.'

The look of disbelief as I refuse is startling. He shakes his head and nods in the direction of the trodden path leading up to the church on top. Once we get halfway up, the crosses begin to appear, varying in size from a few centimetres to well over a metre. By the time we get to the church, which is a tremendously picturesque, wooden building in the typical style of the Orthodox faith, crosses peep out at us from everywhere. It's a visual feast, and Piotr takes me through the woods to the fields at the back where more crosses have been planted randomly, scattered around like toothpicks; some are old and gnarled, others still smelling of fresh resin.

Here lies three hundred years of faith, faith based on a miracle. I will say one thing for the Poles – after all they've been through, they certainly have faith. You can be cynical about it, but it is a sign of a strong human spirit to retain such faith in the face of endless suffering. Or you could, of course, take the view that it is the suffering itself that induces their faith.

The rain is coming down hard again as we walk back through the thick pine woods. With the wind thrashing the tops of the trees, the offer of a cup of tea is sounding a bit more enticing. When we get there, Piotr's mother is bent over in the garden at the front of the house, fiddling with some plants buried in the soggy ground. I think it's lettuce, but whatever it is, five minutes later it's sitting on the kitchen counter as she cuts a loaf of bread between her breasts.

The home is basic, as you would expect here. Having taken off my boots, I sit at the table opposite the door and try to take it all in without appearing rude. A large stove burns away in the far corner, where Piotr is boiling a kettle. His mother stands on my right cutting the bread at the sink, while on my left at the end of the table under a lamp, a handful of newborn chickens prance around in a cardboard box. The room is warm despite the whole house being made of wood, and the smell from the chickens in the box blends somehow with the strong tea just put on the table to give the type of odour you can grab. It's not unpleasant, it's just country.

Down come the sandwiches. Thick bread like the heel of a boot, freshly torn lettuce with traces of muck and meat from the arse of a fat Polish pig. Perfect. Cold hands on a hot mug and the strong taste of ham, the glow from the stove and the beating of the wind-driven rain on the hollow wooden walls. It is at times like this that you want to drop out of the race. They have everything here, she tells me. All the food they can eat is either running around outside or waits to be lifted out of the earth, while life beyond this pleasant little microcosm goes on at a pace that would shorten the lives of these people by half. And what the hell for, I wonder?

I sit there with the family for at least an hour, the father coming in from the yard to join us, bowing slightly and offering his hand. The mother goes through the family history in some detail. She eventually urges Piotr to take out the photo album, something which often happens when you sit with Polish families. While going through the photos, Piotr goes into his room and returns with a box of inexpensive chocolates. It was his birthday yesterday, the mother tells me, as he offers me one. There are only about four gone from the box and he has had them a day. I wonder how many times he has been given a box of chocolates.

Eventually, Piotr tells me it is time to get the train; he will show me where the timetable is. It's sunny again when we step outside, growing warm, and the smell of wet grass and steam hangs in the air. Piotr takes me up the hill and across the track to a bank on the far side. The station is up here, he tells me.

Climbing to the top of the bank, I'm greeted by an old woman, scarf on head, sitting on an empty crate beside a cow. The 'station' turns out to be her house – on the wall in her porch is nailed a timetable carved from a piece of wood. I am sure I would have found it eventually.

If time moves too fast, visits to places like this appear to slow it down for a while. Sentimental that may be, but it's true. Normal days for modern man are not made up of working to live. You live to work, and the result is wealth. Going out with a bucket to the water pump will mean that the cup of tea you make will be cherished. Running out of the train station and grabbing a take-out on the way to the office will mean it won't be. It is that simple.

When I got back home that evening, I remember feeling a bit emotional about the whole experience. Hospitality like that is such a rare and odd experience that it is bound to leave an impression. This mood doesn't last very long – it is quickly driven out by the real world. A taste, though, is enough to leave a tinge of regret.

I promised myself to go back there once more before leaving for good. The truth is though, I grew afraid to. Something would have changed that would ruin it for me – a bus stop, a new platform, a shop, something. I'm better off just keeping the one image. Some time later, however, I sent the family a postcard – the mother had given me their address and made me promise I would send her son a card from home. I hope they got it, I really do.

Beer Barrel Polka

If places like Grabarka represent the Poland of old, travel to the west is the polar opposite. The German influence is immediate, those who live there tending to speak to you in German rather than English upon hearing you're a foreigner. BMWs are everywhere. Stylish restaurants, chain stores, designer names and top brands on billboards; it is obvious why we were sent as volunteers to the east rather than to the west.

In the second year of our stay, myself and a few of the lads in the group got an urge to buy a bar. It was a bit mad, one of those ideas actually conceived in a bar. But it was a bar in Minsk, opened by a student, which gave us the idea. If he could do it, so could we. Only better. That was the motivation.

The other bars in the town at that time were rarely visited. There was a café that was too full of students and closed at ten o'clock. There was a bar at the bottom of a block of flats that had two pool tables and plastic patio furniture. That was the spot I frequented with the 'po-maturalne' students who I had grown close to in the first year. It was an awful place, but it was a bar. The bar lady was very friendly, and gave you bread and 'smalec' with every round. 'Smalec' was basically a thick fat spread that a lot of the alcoholics ate. It helped line your stomach. You would see them early in the morning buying a bottle of spirits, some bread and a little, margarine-sized pack of smalec. The sad fact was that they were saving money on food to buy drink, and lining their gut with this stuff instead.

There was also the café place that I had avoided on my second day, which catered for older people and had a dance of sorts on a Sunday. You could get breaded pork chops there after a few beers and the bar ladies, dressed in flowery aprons, would warn you against drinking cold beer in the winter. Actually, they would almost refuse to serve it. They would point at your throat and offer a tepid bottle or, better still, hot beer with cloves.

The bar that inspired us, though, was a dirty, festering dive. There were no doors on the toilets, and the cubicles for men and women were right next to each other. That's the first image that comes flooding back, as images of that nature would. If a girl wished to pee, a friend or boyfriend stood where the door should have been and blocked the view. Men didn't bother trying to block the view, some-times using the sink. I've seen bars in the States that employ similar tactics when it comes to their toilets, but that's mostly to prevent drug users from injecting them-selves. In this bar, it was simply because the owner wasn't arsed hanging doors.

Some of the insane antics that went on in that bar have long since been obliterated from memory. Many nights went on until six in the morning, with Sunday creeping in through cracks in the grubby windows. With a floor caked in filth, a toilet gurgling in excrement and a rowdy mob every weekend, its heinous reputation was smeared on the feet of all who passed through it, and spread thereafter throughout the town like a plague.

Some of the characters that haunted the place, I'm convinced, were merely bodies separated from a mind cremated by meths. Descartes would have loved to have met them. Dark eyes with black rings like tractor tyres gazed from hollow corners of the pub. Gaunt faces, cheekbones hoovered into dry mouths, barely a sentence passing their lips. Christ, to think I was among them as a teacher.

Strangely though, I never saw any trouble there. Some of the more rebellious students frequented this dump also, and for a while we all rolled out the same door in the same state on a Sunday morning. There were a few 'po-maturalne' students who I went there with regularly. They made more of an effort in class as a result – most of them anyhow. So I figured that I was doing a good service by going out and getting hammered with them. Anyway, I needed the company.

Of course, I was 'advised' not to go there by some of the teachers when they found out. The director said nothing, and the vice director, who was quite fond of a tipple herself, thought it was a great idea for me to mix with the students as much as possible. But some of the English teachers were concerned. That pub had a bad name and my reputation simply wouldn't recover.

They were probably right. You can drink a lot and get away with it in Poland, but there were many with serious drinking problems from which there seemed to be no going back. The price of vodka didn't help. There were nights with Poles where a serious, dangerous amount of drink was consumed. We all had the tales to tell, and they weren't even funny.

This particular bar, perhaps inevitably, didn't last very long. After a few months it changed hands. As it attempted to clean itself up, the old crowd left or died off. Finally, it was closed down as a condemned building. The name of the bar, by the way, was 'Beirut'.

Deciding that Poles didn't know how a good bar should look or how it should be run, myself and Keith, a friend from Belfast, saw a viable business opportunity. After a bit of research, we decided to visit a town called Wroclaw, in the west of Poland, to see if we could find a premises. Lord knows what we were thinking about. It was a ridiculous idea, as Wroclaw is one of the richer cities in the country and has plenty of bars already. Even if it hadn't, a group of lads on APSO volunteer money would never have been able to afford a lease, and if APSO had found out there would have been hell to pay. APSO send volunteers to other countries so that the natives can benefit from our 'skills' and go on to make good livings for themselves, not vice versa. While our intentions at the time we came over were noble, we were a bit warped twelve months later, and were quite prepared to build for the future, providing a valuable service to the community at the same time.

Getting into the station in Wroclaw late on a Thursday night after a seven-hour journey, we check into the nearest hotel, directly across the way. It's a bit dingy, but fine. We book three beds, since we've arranged to meet another friend, Paul, off a later train at about 12.30am.

It is some time in March, and a cold night. Poland is balancing on the cusp between winter and spring, always the worst period since you never know what kind of weather you'll be assaulted by. Myself and Keith head out for a bite to eat and a couple of beers, finding a bar eventually but no food. The first thing we notice is the price of everything, almost double what we're used to paying in the east.

At midnight we leave the bar, which is closing anyway, and turn back to the station. It is bitterly cold now, with a harsh wind and biting sheets of sleet. We're not talking much, since we're both thinking the same thing. A bar of our own is a pipe dream, another one of mine that will have to go up in smoke. What is more, we're here for the weekend and it's not a cheap city. We should really just go home.

The train is delayed. No one can tell us why, so we'll just have to wait. Train stations in Poland are not good places to wait, day or night. Warsaw Central, for example, although well-serviced, has a few dodgy corridors and passageways that are a vision straight from the pages of a horror book. Junkies hang around like vampires, clawing at passers by, and smells ranging from hotdogs to urine float in the air.

Wroclaw station is not much better, at least, not at night. It is a long building with gaudy shops and cafés parked along either side, mostly closed now save a few rudimentary hangouts selling beer and coffee. We make for one that has a good view of the information board and get beer in plastic glasses.

The place is submerged in drunkards, and after an hour we're beginning to fit right in. Nobody hangs around stations at this time except drunks, and nobody goes into the station bars except drunks. Leaning on a plastic table, we stare out at the wind blowing about a few papers and patches of sleet.

A drunkard parks himself beside us and begins to chat. I like talking to these guys sometimes. They all have a story to tell, and most of them, at some point in their lives, had a place to call home. Keith swears in his sharp Northern accent and heads to the information desk, leaving me to chat with the drunk. It turns out he's a fisherman from Kaliningrad, a corner port belonging to Russia that no one in Poland seems to know anything about. Nor do they want to, but that's another story. The guy offers me a job on a fishing boat, but I decline. There can't be too many creatures left alive in the Baltic.

At about 2am, the train comes in and there's no sign of Paul. Tired, cold and drunk, we go to bed.

Friday morning isn't so cold, but the dark sky looks swollen with rain. During a McDonald's breakfast, we browse through a local paper and discover the address of an agency that deals with leasing. An hour's rambling finds us parked at a desk in front of a very attractive lady, with Keith trying to explain in Polish that we're here to find a vacant building to open a pub.

She's not taking us seriously. To begin with, we're not dressed very well, with Keith in a striped anorak and me in a black docker's jacket. On top of that, we're both hungover, our eyes pinched up from the cold wind and the alcohol. We react with shock at a price she finally gives us, then wander away, feeling like a pair of eejits.

The rest of the day is spent touring the city, wishing we lived here instead of in the east. After several hours of brooding, we go on a pub-crawl to reinforce the fact that we'll never own one ourselves. Then we almost get into a spot of trouble.

Some time after one in the morning, we're drifting around the main square looking for another drinking den and we approach a taxi driver for a recommendation. Asking us what it is we want, the word 'girls' is blurted out unconsciously. A strip bar or something similar is what we had in mind, a bit of harmless fun to raise the spirits.

We climb into the taxi, after the driver – clad in tracksuit and gold chains – assures us he knows a good place. The tracksuit and gold chains are the uniform here for thugs and 'mafia', with most of the taxis run by the mafia in the larger cities. You usually get ripped off if you land in one of these, but, unless you do something drastic, that's about the worst that will happen. Of course, if you try and argue the fee at the end of your journey, you're liable to find yourself surrounded by a dozen more tracksuit-clad thugs who have been radioed in.

We wind through a few back streets of the old town and head out onto a main road. The further we go, the more suspicious we become, as the town seems to disappear behind us and the road ahead becomes drenched in darkness. 'Christ,' Keith begins, 'I knew it, we're fucked now.'

Despite his fears, I'm not that worried. I have a feeling I know where we're heading, and begin to think it's funny. Maybe it's due to Keith's background, but he has convinced himself that we're going to be robbed and shot. After half an hour, we pull over on the edge of a quiet road and stop outside a large house. Now my mood changes. Shaped like a cardboard box, two square windows stare out from the top of the building, lit from somewhere in the background by a pair of seedy red lights. It's like the Amityville Horror. The driver steps out and I expect him to a have a cloven foot, just like that story my ma used to tell me about the devil. But he doesn't, he has a pair of imitation Adidas.

He leads us into the hall. We pay him and are met by a sleazy-looking guy with a goatee beard. A curtain is pulled back, revealing a large, sombre room that smells of dirty sex, cleverly disguised by cheap incense. About ten girls sit in a line, gazing up at us from a balding couch against the near wall. One of them has one of her breasts hanging out and smiles as we run past them, towards a tiny bar in the corner. At this point, of course, the laughter sets in. We were already well hammered before we got there, and are now suffering from a dose of nerves. I could pretend and tell a typical sailor story, tattoos and all. But I'll tell the boring truth instead.

In Poland, organised criminals, who like to call themselves 'mafia', import women from other Central and Eastern European countries, as well as from Russia. They also export Polish girls to the West. This arrangement was, of course, aided by the break up of the Soviet states in the early nineties. The Polish mafia is taken seriously here, although most are really nothing more than common gangsters. When it comes down to sorting out the men from the boys, it's the Russians who have the balls.

However, these Polish gangs still run a good business. The girls they bring in are generally aged between sixteen and twenty, many arriving in Poland in the hope that it can be used as a springboard to the West. Once they arrive, ostensibly to work as waitresses or hotel staff, their documents are taken from by the traffickers, who force them into prostitution on the pretence that the costs of their passage have gone up.

For many of these poor unfortunates, the closest they'll get to the West is the motorway, where they can be seen in the spring and summer sporting tight bicycle shorts and shiny tops, hitching a lift. It is a rather ridiculous sight – lines of heavily made-up girls standing along the road near the woods, sticking their bums out at passing cars. But it's also very tragic.

One area of Poland, Zielona Gora, has a twenty-kilometre road that cuts through the forests close to the German border. For the Germans, this is a Mecca for the sex trade – the price of a girl on this side is probably three times less than they would pay in Germany. Gubin, a town in this area, has a population of 15,000, together with fourteen escort agencies working round the clock. The women here are predominantly from the former Soviet states. Most have obtained legal residence permits and are relatively well educated. According to the police, they ply their trade by their own free will. If there exists a ladder of success in this business, then working in a top-class escort agency is fairly close to the top.

There are some who make it to the West, but not on their intended career path. Having been 'trained' in Poland, many are sold on to brothels in Germany or Holland for a sum that can be as little as $250 and as high as $4,500, depending on their appearance and well-being. Many of these girls come from very impoverished backgrounds and will already have suffered hardships. They mightn't last very long. What happens to them in countries like Holland or Germany when they are finally no use doesn't bear thinking about.

Their services in the West, incidentally, fetch about $45 to $90 a pop, from which the woman gets a very small proportion. If you cross the border into Poland to pick up one of these roadside girls, the most you'll pay is about $25 with condoms, $45 without. To think a girl is willing to risk her life for an extra $20 is an example of how desperate they are.

The type of club that we had envisaged going to is quite common throughout the country, essentially lap-dance and strip clubs that have a regular strip show if you don't wish to get too close. Some are seedier than others, but we used to look at it as entertainment for the boys abroad, and rarely considered that some of the girls may have been there against their will. We would go and spend hours sipping vodka and gazing at girls, many of whom would previously only have visited our dreams. These clubs are mostly run by thugs, who are very easy to spot. When you enter the club, they're the ones at the largest table, surrounded by food, girls, and bottles of vodka and dressed in tracksuits and gold pendants. You would want to be a brave man to try anything, but by the same token they try and run the clubs with some degree of efficiency.

The thought that this brothel was mafia run went through our heads that night. If it was we were in a spot of trouble. There were no tracksuits around, but that didn't mean much. We sank lower and lower on the bar stools and broke into a fit of laughter, especially since the girl with her breast hanging out was parading herself in front of us.

Goatee comes up and asks if we want a drink before 'going upstairs'. A beer costs about four quid, about five times the amount we've been paying all night. Goatee then says that to 'go upstairs' will cost us three million. Back then, that was about seventy quid, almost a month's wages for a teacher. His girls must be good. I gaze over at them on the couch and they stare back at us. I wonder which one it would be, if I had to. But whatever about having a giggle or a grope at a girl swinging her breasts over your vodka in a strip bar, I felt too young, too innocent and too poor to be going upstairs to a smelly mattress. Keith, still in paranoid mode, suddenly leans forward on the bar and, with his head in his hands, tries to explain.

'Look, we're Irish,' he blurts out, 'and I think we've made a mistake here. We don't want to go upstairs, we want to go home. We're really, really sorry if we've wasted your time.'

Goatee stares for a minute, then he laughs. This is not a mafia place, he tells us, though most are. It is his private house and the girls get a good commission. They are screened regularly, thus the higher charges. As he speaks, a large, stiff-looking guy strolls in and, without even getting a drink, grabs one of the girls by the hand and disappears through the curtain. 'German,' Goatee says. After chatting for a while he orders a taxi for us and we leave, bidding the girls a goodnight on the way.

The next night is a repeat of the first, only we don't go near any taxis. After three nights we arrive back in Warsaw, having spent two months' worth of our Polish wages on expensive bars and tricky situations. The idea of a bar is, of course, down the toilet, leaving a large, black space in our futures that neither of us really knows how to fill. But then, none of us had any idea of our futures when we came here. In many ways that was the beauty of it.

By the close of that year, though, it was decision time. It was 1996, and a lot was happening back in Ireland. People were picking up houses, securing good jobs, investing money and settling down. The repercussions of being away when the Celtic Tiger was beginning to roar was something that none of us could have anticipated. Those who acted on instinct – like Keith, who was depressed after that Wroclaw trip anyway – and made the decision to pack up and leave, ultimately made a wise choice. He now works in an estate agency in Leeds. Whenever I met him thereafter his reaction was always one of disbelief.

'So you're still in Poland? In the same town? What the hell are you doing there? Get your act together. When you get home you'll realise that teaching English abroad is not going to stand to you.'

It worried me greatly at the time.

Most of the original group had by now made the decision to bail out. They were replaced with others from Ireland, as APSO deemed that the project had so far been a success. At least, they were still getting requests from schools to supply more teachers.

Those of us who remained did so for various reasons, a common one being the irresistible draw of Polish girls, or in some cases, Polish men. From the original group of nineteen that came over, five in total got married. Another friend of mine from the second group also eventually married, making a total of six. But to prove that Polish girls were more attractive than Polish men, four out of the seven guys tied the great Gordian knot, compared to only two of the dozen or so girls.

At that point, I had requested an extension of my contract, after much thought and some very long nights. Asha's doctor in Warsaw had been given the shoulder at the end of year one, once I had sent a letter to APSO requesting an extension to my contract. Now, at the end of year two, after long nights of soul searching, I did the same again.

With some of my close Irish friends gone, life was a bit tougher. I had some decisions to make about a career, but had no real options. I eventually reasoned that I was as happy here teaching as I was going to be anywhere, even though some of the conditions were miserable. Misery though, is a relative state, and can be tolerated when you've knowingly put yourself in a situation. I never wanted much when I came here, and I never got much.

What I got, though, I called home. I found myself quite contented with my measure, and was growing to love the place I lived in. It is amazing how a lack of luxury can make the simplest of pursuits so pleasurable. After two years I still had no television, but found that a stereo, a decent selection of CDs, a bunch of books and a fridge with a few beers in it can make a man content for a time.

I confess to later getting a television, so that I could get hold of some videos in English. And to be honest, any more than a couple of weeks without company and depression would set in. But I was living among people who had less than I had, and if they managed, then so could I. I had become friendly with many of them and had settled into their way of life. Although I moaned about some of the day-to-day chores I had to endure, I basically had no impulse to leave.

Largely cut off from life at home, relying only on a weekly paper and with no internet, I began to immerse myself in books about Poland, whenever I could get my hands on something in English. My students recommended a few novels. I read histories of the country and books by Czeslaw Milosz and Ryszard Kapuscinski – brilliant stuff. I read histories of the Second World War, particularly on the Holocaust, a subject that seems to fascinate so many people. That it does is probably a good thing, because it means it will never be forgotten. But so much of Poland contains vestiges of the Holocaust that it is impossible to avoid the subject.

I got hold of a book by Daniel Goldhagen called *Hitler's Willing Executioners*, which had a photo of Jews being rounded up in the Jewish Quarter of the very town I was living in. The photo shows the Jews being forced to play leapfrog before being put into waiting vans. The Jewish Quarter had been only a stone's throw away from where I was in the internat, and nearby was a Jewish cemetery. There were now very few Jews still in Minsk.

Asha's father had a long spell in hospital around this time, with an illness that would eventually lead to his death at the tragically young age of fifty-seven. One evening when we went to visit him he was beside a very old man who chatted away and joked, despite the fact that the hospital was grim and his condition appeared grimmer still. He told us that he had spent years imprisoned in Soviet gulags and the physical extremes were now really taking their toll.

Asha's grandfather, she once told me when I brought up the subject of the War, had also been imprisoned in Russia, where he was tortured. He managed to escape from the train that was bound for the gulags of Siberia and made it all the way home on foot in mid-winter. He got to the family home, but collapsed in the house and died from a heart attack very soon afterwards.

You could pick any student in any class and doubtless they would have a tragedy behind them. However, you generally didn't hear about it unless you asked. Silent, strong, tough, resilient people are the Poles. I learned to look at them differently, and look at human nature differently, after some time in their country.

The suffering that these people had gone through, during and after the Second World War, eventually became something of an obsession of mine. I felt compelled to learn more about it.

This Way for the Gas

Before the war, there was a young Polish man who had a fine career as a writer ahead of him. His name was Tadeusz Borowski, and his short life was a tough one.

Born in the Ukraine in 1922 to Polish parents, his father was transported to one of the worst labour camps – the White Sea Canal, above the Arctic Circle – for having participated in a Polish military organisation in the First World War. His mother was sent to Siberia.

In 1932, his father was among prisoners exchanged for communists held in Poland and the family was eventually repatriated in Warsaw. Tadeusz was sent to a boarding school run by Franciscans. When the war broke out he was only seventeen.

During the German occupation, college and school were forbidden to Poles, a 'sub-species' who didn't warrant a good education. The Nazi jackboots had hammered resistance into the ground within a matter of days in the west of the country, when they invaded on September 1, 1939, and the plan with regard to Poland soon became obvious: the educated class was to be exterminated, the country colonised. The east of the country was well looked after by Stalin, who invaded on September 17, deporting thousands to prisons in Siberia, and massacring the elite in the forests of Bielorussia.

Borowski studied in underground classes and later worked as a night watchman and stockboy for a firm that sold building materials. This meant he had a work card and could avoid being sent to the Reich to make up for the labour shortage there.

The underground press in Warsaw during the war was prolific and extremely hardworking, with dozens of leaflets, such as translations of radio broadcasts from the West, appearing each day from various sources. Borowski published his first volume of poetry, *Wherever the Earth*, underground in a rudimentary form. But it was enough to incriminate him. A few weeks later, he was arrested. He had with him at the time a copy of Huxley's *Brave New World*. This was a bad move. A copy of *Mein Kampf* might have saved him, but he wasn't in Paris and he wasn't Beckett.

From a prison in Warsaw he was moved to Auschwitz, and from there, in 1944, to Dachau in Germany. His stories, which were later published under the title *This Way to the Gas, Ladies and Gentlemen*, are sordid tales of life in the concentration camp. The world he portrays and the figures fighting for survival in it, are not only rugged, naked, fragile and devoid of flesh, but are also devoid of any scrap of moral or altruistic inclination. People are stripped of any feeling but that of the base, animal instinct to survive. The other creatures – the dogs, rats and lice that crawl over every page – walk hand-in-hand with the victims. Life, through Borowski's lens, doesn't care a damn who it lives in, a Jew or a rat or a louse.

In 1951, having survived 'the chimneys', Borowski gassed himself in his flat. He wasn't yet thirty.

It is a bleak read. And it was one of the first books I read, having asked the girls in school which books from Polish authors I was likely to pick up in English. This book had become compulsory reading for the students on the school curriculum.

Majdanek was the first camp I visited. The second biggest camp in Poland, it lies just outside the town of Lublin, where we all stayed in the first year. I will admit a certain amount of ignorance about the place when we went to visit in that first week in the country, even playing travel scrabble on the bus with one of the girls on the way there.

Most people were just yawning and gazing out at the scenery as we passed through the town and out onto the main road towards the camp. There were the usual comments when some of the more conscientious girls said they weren't going to go in at all – 'Go on, it'll be a gas.'

None of us really knew what to expect. Schindler's List had been showing at the time, so the subject of Poland and the Holocaust was fresh in our minds at least, but not all of us were aware of the whole history. I remember turning the corner on the coach and suddenly being faced with the camp in the distance.

The joking stopped instantly and all heads turned to stare. It resembled one of those evil castles in animated fantasy cartoons. The reaction was the same all over the bus, the scene tapping straight into childhood reserves of bad feelings.

Dark towers loomed out of the field, bowing down on the still and eerie interior, which was surrounded by a raging mess of barbed wire. Within lay the butcher's yard, most of it still intact. The hanging posts. The gas chambers. The crematorium. The prisoners' blocks. It was motionless, inert, deadly quiet, yet still seemed to exude a vicious, punishing energy. It looked, in fact, as if it had only been abandoned yesterday.

There was a film, followed by a guided tour which took us around the camp, through the gas chambers, the prisoners' compounds, the punishment blocks and finally the crematorium at the back, the fierce chimney still blackened and whole. A vast mountain of ash lay next to the crematorium, sheltered by a roof to form a memorial. The history of the camp was vividly described by the old Polish guide, who had lost some of his own family within those walls. He stood in the gas chambers, the walls still stained, and went through details of how long it took for the gas to kill a person and what exactly happened.

Wood is supposedly a good retainer of human energy, and standing there in the wooden prisoners' blocks, it was as if someone ran a cube of ice down your spine or a comb over the back of your neck. But Majdanek is only one of many such places in Poland. The country really is littered with reminders.

Not only did Poland have the highest number of Nazi concentration camps of any country – one commentator put the figure at 5,800, which would include holding camps and transit camps of all sizes and shapes, but camps nonetheless – but each and every town you pass through bears scars of the Holocaust and of the War. As a work camp, Majdanek had a mortality rate higher than any other camp – except the extermination camps – with forty percent of victims being gassed or shot on arrival, and most of the rest dying from starvation, exhaustion and disease within weeks. Of almost 500,000 people who passed through the gates of Majdanek, 360,000 never left.

It was in Poland that the answer to the 'Jewish question', which had been lingering on the lips of Europe for centuries, was answered. It became a slaughterhouse. Poland, by the twentieth century, was the 'crown' of World Jewry. King Kazimierz, Poland's great King who reigned in the fourteenth century, had granted refuge and special privileges to Jews, who settled in great numbers during his reign, a time when Jews were victimised in just about every other country in Europe. But Poland would ultimately pay the price. Hitler wished to close the Jewish chapter once and for all, and Poland was the place to do it.

The country was perfect, not only to deal with Polish Jewry, but Jews all over Central and Eastern Europe. It was centrally located geographically and had a widespread railroad infrastructure, together with a large supply of rolling stock, which could easily feed the rest of Europe. The great English historian on Polish events, Norman Davies, has an apt title for the country: God's Playground. Stalin called it a crossroads.

Hitler's fervent anti-Semitism was really without basis – at least, any basis that anyone can find. The myths of his Jewish background have no foundation, as he was brought up a Catholic. Many commentators believe that Hitler's plans for world domination were subordinate to those for the annihilation of the Jews. For if he really believed the Jews to be so powerful, could he not have used their skills for his nation, since many were able scientists? But he didn't.

Instead of concentrating the German army on making up for its failure to take Moscow in 1941, he used up large quantities of supplies and highly trained divisions for the murder of innocent people who weren't even the legitimate enemy. Even when the tide had turned in 1944, and the war was as good as lost, Hitler continued to transport Jews from Hungary and Greece.

Hitler had at his mercy about 500,000 Jews in Germany, and about 200,000 more once Austria was annexed in 1938. It was then he turned to Poland.

Hitler's crusade didn't only involve the Jews, of course. As soon as he came to power he began his euthanasia spree in Germany. Invalids and the elderly were wiped out, though this campaign was suspended eventually. Gypsies were rounded up and killed or taken to the camps. By 1945, only 5,000 gypsies remained in Germany. After Germany's walkover in Poland in 1939, he immediately ordered the massacre of the Polish elite. Two-and-a-half million officers and intellectuals from various backgrounds were executed, ensuring the Polish populace had less chance of being trained and educated by their own.

The dual camp of Auschwitz-Birkenau is probably the one with the most familiar name to people, and I visited the place several times. I remember one year in the town of Oswiecim – Polish for Auschwitz – a peculiar and rather tragic battle of a different kind was raging.

Most visitors to Auschwitz are surprised to find a town there at all. But there was, and still is, a town with a population of about 50,000. Life goes on there as it does in any other town. But how normal can a town be with the ghosts of over a million victims haunting it? Two arguments are constantly cropping up.

There are those who feel that life should continue, and wish to see bars, clubs and cafés spring up as they do everywhere else. One entrepreneur even wanted to open a 'social club' – a brothel, basically. Others feel that the town should respect the memory of its victims by retaining an air of calm and peace, and so object to the idea of bars and cafés and the like.

The second argument is also about sensitivities. The Jews erect Stars of David in memory of the victims of

Auschwitz-Birkenau. The Poles erect crosses to pray for the non-Jewish victims of Auschwitz-Birkenau. One cross in particular, a twenty-six-foot cross blessed by the Pope in 1979 and moved from Birkenau to Auschwitz, became a huge sticking point. The Jews saw it as an outrage, an attempt to 'Christianise' the Holocaust. It is as if a decision has to be made over who suffered more, and who therefore deserves greater symbols. There was an international agreement to avoid symbols of any sort at Auschwitz, but that was ignored.

Auschwitz-Birkenau was officially a camp for Jews. We can establish that as a fact quite easily, because it came from the horse's mouth. The camp commandant, Rudolf Hoss, said so himself: 'Auschwitz became a Jewish camp. It was a collecting place for Jews, exceeding in scale anything previously known.'

The mortality rate in the camp for Jews was higher than for other prisoners – Poles, Russian prisoners of war, Gypsies, other European nationals and anti-socials (such as German prisoners, homosexuals and Jehovah's Witnesses). Jews who arrived in the camp would already have been subject to harsh conditions in the ghettos, where they had to do the hardest work and received starvation rations. In the camps, they were not allowed to receive parcels and were thus deprived of any chance of getting extra food. They were also excluded from any privileged positions in the camp. These positions, such as camp 'capos', tasked with keeping order, were given to more brutal and mostly 'green' (criminal) prisoners. These capos were notorious for their sadism against their fellow prisoners.

Other privileged positions were in the camp Sonder-kommando – where Borowski worked, managing to stay alive because of it. This unit was in charge of unloading the prisoners from the ramp upon arrival, separating them from their goods and cremating the bodies after the gas. Because of the nature of their work, they were topped up with rations – especially vodka – and enjoyed better living conditions.

Jews arriving in the camp were separated into those who were fit to work and those who weren't. This decision went against the original order of the immediate destruction of all Jewish transports, which began arriving in January 1942. However, there was a need for more labour in the armaments industry. The elderly and infirm, as well as children and women with children in their arms, went straight to the gas. The rest were put to work, but few lasted longer than several weeks.

In February 1943, a telegram was received by the camp commandant to the effect that all Gypsies should be exterminated. Gypsies from France, Hungary, Poland, Germany and elsewhere began to arrive. The rounding up of Gypsies was in itself an act that only proves the madness of the Nazi regime. For military reasons, certain people are rounded up and used in war as hostages. Even the killing of the elite of societies in time of war can be seen as a strategic act, whether morally justifiable or not. Long before the war, Gypsies were being rounded up and placed in camps as part of the campaign against 'asocials'. Research was being conducted to separate the 'stock' of pure-blooded Gypsy, the direct descendants of the Indo-Germanic race. The idea behind this was, as Hoss puts it, 'to have them registered and preserved as a historical monument'.

After 1942, all other Gypsies were taken to Auschwitz, to be kept there for the duration of the war. However, the regulations governing arrest were ambiguous and caused much confusion among the arresting officers. Many men were arrested despite having been decorated or wounded, because their mothers or grandmothers were not pure-blooded.

A total of 22,667 Gypsies were transported to Birkenau and lived in appalling conditions. As Hoss reports, disease was rife as a result of starvation and exhaustion. Finally, he was ordered to destroy them, which he says was hard on him because they were really like children.

Also brought to Auschwitz were 13,775 Russian prisoners of war. At the last roll-call before the camp was evacuated, there were ninety-two prisoners of war left. Among those shot or gassed immediately were 900 Commissars of the Soviet army. The first trial in using Cyclon B – the official gas of the camps, normally used as insecticide – was in fact carried out against the Russians. It was a success, and came to take the place of exhaust fumes from lorries in the bigger extermination camps.

Russian POWs were always going to be treated badly, since their side hadn't signed the Geneva Convention and refused to grant prisoner-of-war status to captured soldiers. Their food rations in Auschwitz, for example, consisted of a half-litre of soup made from rotten turnips, 300 grams of bread with a small spread of margarine, or fifty grams of sausage. Their condition was like that of zombies, and Hoss mentions cannibalism among other atrocities in the Russian group.

But until early in 1942, the largest group of prisoners was Poles.

The Poles, as they did tirelessly on the outside, were able to organise a camp resistance movement which continued throughout the war. They were largely kept as hostages.

As hostages, they could be shot or hanged in retaliation for attacks against the SS in occupied Poland. In April 1942, for example, over two days, a group of 198 painters, intellectuals, lawyers and other artists were arrested in an artists' café in Krakow in retaliation for the attempted assassination of an SS officer at the airport. 169 were shot at 'death wall' on 27 May.

The Nazis didn't really need hostages behind the wire though. The whole country had been taken hostage, and any resistance was severely punished. In September 1942, a German detachment was ambushed in a place called Talcyn, where they were attempting to trap two resistance fighters. A German sergeant was killed. In a report, the ambush was referred to as a 'cowardly act' and retribution was demanded. The 300 inhabitants of the village were rounded up and the Germans shot seventy-eight of them at the graveyard.

Poles were executed for having read resistance leaflets, or shot randomly in retaliation for any anti-Nazi operation. In 1940, the German governor of Poland set out the Nazi vision. Poland was to become 'a gigantic work camp, where everything that means power and independence is in the hands of the Germans'. No Pole would 'rise to a rank higher than foreman', or ever receive a higher education. The Polish State would never be restored.

The Polish underground movement, as early as 1942, was working round the clock to communicate the horrors of the Nazi regime – at great risk to themselves, their families and Polish prisoners who could be shot in retaliation.

In the summer of 1942, Jan Karski, a twenty-eight-year-old courier for the resistance movement in Poland, was sent by the Government-in-exile to report on the activities of the Nazis. He went to Warsaw and visited the infamous ghetto. He witnessed also the rounding up of Jews into cattle carts for transport to camps. He met two Jewish leaders of underground organisations, who pleaded with him to tell authorities about the fate of the Jews.

He met the foreign secretary in London, along with other officials. He was told by Lord Selbourne, then in charge of operations to help anti-Nazi movements, 'During the First World War, rumours spread all over

Europe that German soldiers in Belgium liked to catch Belgian babies and crush their skulls against the wall. We knew those rumours weren't true, but we didn't do anything to stop them. They were good for the morale of the people.'

Karski had also visited President Roosevelt. 'I am convinced, Mr President,' he said, 'that there is no exaggeration in the accounts of the plight of the Jews. Our Underground authorities are absolutely sure that the Germans are out to exterminate the entire Jewish population of Europe.'

In 1998, the decision was made to remove the smaller crosses from Auschwitz, but to leave the large one that had been blessed by the Pope. The Stars of David remain. As for the Gypsies, Russian Orthodox, Jehovah's Witnesses, atheists and everyone else, they get nothing.

Letters from Poland

It was roughly halfway through my third year when I managed to get a slot on the English-language newspaper for Poland and Central Europe, the *Warsaw Voice*. I happened to meet the English editor, an American guy called Nathan, in a pub one night. After yapping for a while, we arranged a meeting to discuss some of the scribbling that I had been up to as a cure for boredom.

The *Warsaw Voice* was started in 1988, at a time when a lot of underground literature and press was being produced, but had since become a more general paper. It was the only English-language paper until general listings magazines began to appear in the late 1990s, once Poland had opened up enough sufficiently to warrant their appearance.

The editor of the *Warsaw Voice*, Magda, a really decent lady who was so supportive as an editor, was persuaded by Nathan to include a reporter living outside Warsaw, describing the snow, meat that wasn't chopped, the doctor's surgery and other matters that must have seemed a howl. I was happy to do it for them. I needed something to augment my income and also to alleviate the day-to-day tedium of small-town life. I also had a need to write stuff that was light and humorous, to balance what I was reading. Every week I compiled a column on daily issues, also writing a few other articles when the need arose. One of these was on the Holy Mountain in Grabarka.

Mostly my pieces were well-received, although at times there were those who took a dim view of a foreigner criticising their country. I didn't aim to be negative. Some of my writing was cathartic, but most of it was just about life in the country at the time, reflecting the changes, the problems in transition and some of the peculiarities that I happened to find interesting or amusing. As to why a foreigner should have been doing this, well, it was after all an English-language paper and much of its readership was made up of expats.

The following year, I was given an opportunity to work part-time on the national radio station, Polski Radio. It had a section called Radio Polonia, which broadcasted worldwide in seven languages on Polish developments, foreign policy, news and so on. The station began its life in 1936. It went off air during the war, naturally, before resuming in 1945. It was popular all over Eastern Europe and Russia, and its English-language services had a large listenership in Canada, oddly enough, where a lot of Polish emigrants lived. The station seemed keen to have a moaner like myself reporting for the nation on rural development.

I also secured a few classes in a language school in Warsaw, which helped to line the pocket a bit. Even though this was the late 1990s, I was still only receiving about a hundred and fifty pounds a month as a teacher in a State school. The Polish currency had now been stabilised and new denominations introduced, so you didn't even feel like a millionaire anymore. Inflation, while not going through the roof, was also forcing those on the minimum wage to find ways of earning extra money.

Most teachers took up extra lessons, either in their own homes or in the private schools that were springing up all over the place, even in Minsk. People were more aware of the benefits of learning a foreign language apart from Russian, and parents were prepared to spend a bit of extra cash on private lessons. I was plagued to do likewise, and at times gave in. But I dreaded teaching privately in my own home. I also hated taking money from local people and finally decided that I would not do private lessons at home at all. I took classes in Warsaw instead. In one week, I could earn more than I earned in a month in Minsk, doing half the hours.

Fridays now became a day of work rather than leisure. Now, instead of a lie-in, I was up early and into Warsaw with the rest of the commuters on those dreadful trains. Around that time, they began renovating the lines out from Warsaw and the trains became subject to all sorts of delays. An hour's journey could turn into two or three. But it was a good sign all the same, a sign that things were finally being done out here. The towns outside the main cities were being looked at and gradually improved, at least when it came to infrastructure. Small companies also began operating private bus services, a Godsend. They used the old buses, so it was hardly comfort travel, but on intercity routes the standard was remarkably good.

My first stop on a Friday, at ten o'clock, was at the studios of Radio Polonia. I worked there until lunchtime or on into the afternoon, before going out to the offices of the *Warsaw Voice* to file weekly copy. Then it was off to an English language school to teach a three-hour advanced English class. After that I'd be into Ollie Morgan's Irish bar for a feed of beer.

When I began working in the radio station, besides having a 'roving report' from rural and suburban Poland, one of my tasks was to cover a news story for the lunchtime bulletin. To be honest, I didn't enjoy working in radio very much. There was too much pressure there for my liking, particularly on those news stories. You would arrive in the studios on a Friday morning, have a meeting with a few other journalists and the English-language producer, run through the papers and leads, choose a story, and then go after it.

In a couple of hours you had to translate articles, interview a few people on whatever subject you had chosen, write a news story, edit the interviews for the bulletin, and then record your own voiceovers. There were no computers for editing – everything was done using quarter-inch tape and a razor blade. If you cut out an important quote by mistake and threw it on the floor amongst a spiralling mass of other cuttings, as I often did, you were buggered. More often than not, with three or four minutes to go before airing, I would still be sitting at the editing machine with a razor blade and a mass of tape like knotted hair.

At that stage, Rafal, the producer, a friendly but serious man, would come in and grab everything. 'Tom, there's a lot more pressure working in radio than writing that cozy little column you have in the *Warsaw Voice*,' he would say, while putting everything together with the nimble fingers of a puppeteer. 'Now run, like the wind, down to the studio. You have about forty seconds.'

The stories varied in complexity, but they were all, in my opinion, complex. The first story I had to cover was on Viagra. I remember it well. It was day one and I arrived distinctly nervous. I had also been stopped on the Metro in Warsaw for not having a ticket. The Metro, although its single line was completed in 1995, wasn't much use to commuters, as there was no link to the centre. It finally got that link in 1998 and became the talk of the town.

Radio Polonia was on the line and my first day at work was also my first trip on the Metro. Descending into the station at the centre, however, I discovered there were no ticket machines and, being late, I wasn't bothered to go and look for a kiosk. Sure enough, halfway through the journey, the plain-clothes inspectors got on and nabbed me. These guys love nabbing a foreigner. On the bus that serves the airport they nab you if you don't have two tickets – one for yourself and one for your baggage, believe it or not. On this Friday, they hauled me off the train and show me the fine card, 100zl to be paid within a certain number of days. As I was a foreigner I had to pay up right away.

I didn't have it, and showed my ID to prove that I was actually a resident. They put away the card and said I could pay half – to them, of course. I said I didn't have it, and they said they'd have to take me to the police station. I agreed and began walking out. They stopped me and brought the fine down to 40zl. I said I didn't have it. By the time I reached the steps of the station it was down to 20zl, so I gave it to them, whereupon they swore at me and got on a train going back to the centre. Corruption starts at the very bottom in Poland.

I had only been introduced to the producer of Radio Polonia a week or so previously, through a pal of mine, Barry, who had come over with the second APSO group and lived in a village not far from Minsk. Barry had been a guest on one of the shows for several months, doing a 'Poet's Corner' among other things. As he was now in the middle of his PhD, he had decided to call it a day, citing work pressures as the reason. I think he just got a pain in his arse.

The producer, after a brief meeting, seemed happy to take me on board to fill in. I had no real radio training, aside from a short, part-time course I hadn't even completed some years before. I resigned from that course after about six months because I didn't like the medium of radio. Why I had decided to do something I didn't like in another country was a contradiction I never really tried to resolve.

At the meeting on that first morning, the stories for the day were being discussed and I was asked if I knew anything about Viagra. Very little, was my answer, which was true. It was a new drug at the time and all anybody knew was that it helped you go like the clappers when you popped it. The thing was, people were dying from it in Poland. Heart attacks apparently. Whether this was down to the diet here or the fact that most people got their Viagra on the black market wasn't clear. Either way, they were croaking. I was handed a few Polish newspapers and told to go at it. I could ring a few people from the medical board and get an interview to supplement the story. I could also ring the cops and get some information on the black market.

There is nothing like starting at the deep end. And for the first few weeks I was a drowning man. With the other hacks embedded in their own news stories, I would sit at the tape recorder with a phone book and a scowl, pretending to be sifting through numbers and scribbling furiously on a pad. But as soon as I got a chance, I'd run into the corridor to look for Peter, an English guy who worked there, and beg him for help. Some of the time he bailed me out, but mostly he was too busy himself.

When things were desperate and no interviews could be found, I would grab the portable tape recorder and head off down the corridor to visit a Polish girl who worked for the music department and spoke good English. I would describe the story I was working on, tell her what to say and record it. I think the producer grew suspicious after a while, when this one mysterious girl whose voice boomed out on the airwaves every week happened to be an expert on just about everything.

'Roving reports' were another duty, and once outside the confines of the studio I began to enjoy the radio business more. I would often interview members of the ex-pat community on various issues and put together a short bulletin for one of the magazine programmes. There were also rural reports I did from Minsk, hunting down interviewees in the town. These actually interested the staff in the station, who seemed to regard the town I lived in as another world entirely. Ultimately, they were right, and the people of Minsk were keen to get their voices heard. Whenever I was stuck I would go to the private English school to chat to the students, or at times the teacher. The subjects varied, but the kids always had an opinion that fitted in perfectly with the angle I wanted to cover. Especially when it came to discussing that God-awful Disco Polo.

My time to start winding down came about a year later, after one of the 'Letters from Poland' was pulled by the assistant producer. The 'Letter' was a simple story from Poland, a duty I shared with Peter, and was generally a lighthearted and very doable affair. A very friendly but stressed man, the assistant producer was a sort of intellectual Frank Spencer, always a bit on edge. He was great help if you were stuck, however, and for that I was always grateful.

One morning I was on my way to record one of these 'Letters', this particular one being about the Pope, who had put forward the name of a notorious fascist for Beatification. It was an outrage, and a grave insult to those who had suffered as a consequence of this man's actions during the War. I found it just plain odd that nobody was saying anything about it. It was also, in my view, lucid confirmation that the Pope – who still had many intelligent things to say – was perhaps no longer playing with a full team.

Also, around that time, the Pope was visiting the country for the first time since his visit in 1979. For reasons that nobody could explain, alcohol was banned for the duration of his tour. Even top hotels in Warsaw were forced to remove drinks from their mini-bars, while shops and bars had to cover up whatever stock they had on the shelves.

Lord knows what kind of penalties were to be enforced if anyone was caught serving – a 'fine' most likely – but the ban was upheld by shopkeepers and pub owners who covered the bottles with brown paper and the beer taps with a sock or something similar. I did manage to persuade one poor woman in Minsk to sell me a few cans on the Friday evening of the Pope's visit, telling her I knew her son well. As she did so a police car pulled up outside and I have yet to see blood drain from a face with such velocity. It was a sight to behold. But it was also worrying. The ban was also unconstitutional, and in the country that was first to draw up a constitution in Europe it was quite ironic.

Excuses like 'respect for the Holy Father' were bandied about. This made no sense to me. Were they worried that people would turn up drunk at the masses? More worryingly, the ban was a result of pressure from the Church. It had never gone through proper democratic channels, but nobody questioned that either.

Before I went down to the studio to record my piece, Peter asked me what it was about. 'The Pope,' I answered, and he gave me a stern warning, which I failed to hear properly as I ran out the door. The assistant producer heard him, however, and out he came, running like the hammers of hell, catching up with me just before I got to the studio. He took my paper and went to his office, coming out ten minutes later with a face the colour of chalk.

The following week, Rafal, the producer – a decent fellow who I suspect felt the same way as I did about the whole affair – calmly explained that I must have been insane to attempt to criticise the Pope on the national radio station. He was right. I was stupid. But the *Warsaw Voice* decided to print it. And the main man behind that operation was reportedly Jewish.

It was all good experience, of course, and I was paid well – about five or ten quid a week if I was lucky. But the money wasn't important. It was an enjoyable time overall and it opened up a whole new area for me, eventually driving the fear of broadcasting out of my system. It was also interesting working in Warsaw, a world apart from Minsk. I remember somebody from Warsaw making a joke about me living in Minsk. He laughed and said, 'You must be a real hero out there.' His attitude was that these people, who lived beyond the pale in places like Minsk or further afield in areas such as Grabarka, were simple 'buraks'.

'Burak' is the diminutive of the word for beetroot in Polish and is an amusing but derogatory term for country folk. However, the 'buraks' were those who I had grown closest to here over the few years.

Many of the people in Warsaw were snobbish, as far as I could see. The students in the school I taught in were a whole different breed. They were more worldly-wise definitely. They were far more privileged, of course. But apart from a handful, they were tough cases, demanding, obstinate and difficult to deal with. I suppose they were paying good money. And if the teacher wasn't up to par then it was made known. If a lesson was badly planned, there was no breaking off into a bit of banter about the local markets or the bad train service and having a bit of a laugh. There would be complaints and slaps on the wrists. One day a certain student would just stop coming.

Then you would find him or her attending the classes of another teacher. Or a student might drop in for one or two lessons, scrutinising you from the corner, then decide you were hopeless and not turn up again.

Rural and urban Poland were two different worlds, years apart. But with the infrastructure now growing rapidly as the new millennium approached, it wouldn't stay that way for long. The private buses, the new train lines, the Metros, all brought the small villages in the region I knew as a backwater in 1994, closer to towns like Minsk, Minsk closer to Warsaw and Warsaw closer to cities in the West. It was very clear to anyone there at the time that with membership of the EU on the horizon, all roads would lead out of Poland and into the West, with millions of Poles taking to them.

And It's Off to the Army

He's about seventeen, I'd say. No more. Baggy jeans, short tight hair crowned with a cap and an oversized Diesel T-shirt hanging off his shoulders. J is probably paying about fifty zloty for one period of private lessons. At least, his parents are. Now he has two sessions of forty-five minutes back-to-back. That's about thirty quid and he does it twice a week. The boss has told me that his usual teacher, who is off sick, generally brings in *Newsweek* or something, and they sit around and have a chat about various issues.

That's an expensive chat. It doesn't seem to bother him though. He reclines on the chair, sticks his feet on the one in front and gives me a wide, friendly grin. Suddenly his mobile rings. He excuses himself for a minute while he chats to his mate about last night's party.

When he finally hangs up, he turns to me and tells me about it with a loud guffaw. It was in his parents' second home in the suburbs. There were plenty of girls, plenty of booze and plenty of designer drugs. The folks didn't know, he says with a laugh. They were in the apartment in Warsaw. He concludes his description of the party with a distant gaze and a wistful shake of the head, as memories of three-in-the-bed romps no doubt come flooding back. He's actually a really nice guy. He's pleasant to talk to and has excellent English. So I move onto other things, like his hobbies – besides partying.

For the rest of the day, he explains, he is going shopping to buy some sprays and a few new caps for his graffiti. That's his passion. The sprays come in different colours and the caps vary the thickness of the jet. He has his own insignia and is quite well known around Warsaw as a spray artist.

Then there is a knock on the door. In walks a woman in her fifties in a sandy-coloured fur coat, a host of shopping bags in her hands. To match the coat, her hair has been recently coloured and styled. It sits comfortably on her head like a fresh cream bun. The bags are all from top stores in the city and they're as crisp and stiff as cardboard. Inside them, I imagine, is about five hundred pound's worth of clothing.

'What are you doing here? Your maths tutor is waiting at home for you. And you shouldn't be driving. Where are the keys?'

'They're here in my pocket.'

'Did you not remember – excuse me,' she says then in English as she turns to me to apologise, beginning again in Polish, 'Come straight home after this lesson. Do you hear me?'

She walks out and young J smiles at me.

'That was my mum. I took a car this morning when I got

home and I forgot I had a maths grind as well,' he laughs.

He took *a* car. God knows how many the family has. He double-booked himself for grinds that must have cost a fair bit of money. Then there's his schooling in the private English Institute in Warsaw, his mobile, his graffiti hobby, and all the parties and girls on the side. Some guys have all the luck.

Saturday night in my old local. It was a great spot when it opened, but it started to go downhill within a matter of five or six months. They stopped doing food, the first nail in the coffin. On a Thursday or Friday night you had been guaranteed a good salad and a few grilled chops. There was nowhere else in the town that knew how to do food like it. After the food disappeared, the bottles of imported beer went the same way. Polish beer is fine, but when you're out for the night there comes a point where you have to go on to something lighter. Otherwise you'll just explode.

The final nail in the coffin was the local 'mafia' moving in. The word 'mafia' is becoming increasingly popular around here. People say the word as if referring to some omnipotent deity that exists outside of time and space. But they're simply organised groups that can be broken down into smaller, less organised and unrelated groups. They control regions geographically, whether that means a whole town, a ghetto, a neighbourhood or even a street. The common denominator is that none of them work, but they all have money. In terms of a mafia food chain, these

Minsk thugs were pretty much at the bottom, mere scum-bags with cars and money. A good car in these parts does give its owner a certain amount of prestige though.

In they'd come, demanding a table, locking themselves in the toilet to talk on the phone and generally behaving like arseholes. Eventually, the good customers stopped coming.

This was a good bar, run by a young married couple. Unlike a lot of bar owners in the town they knew how to treat people, as they'd travelled and had both worked abroad. I asked them what had happened to the food, the beer and the live music. It was okay for me and my mates, they said, to come here on the weekend and get hammered until the cows came home. But during the week where are you? We have to get business in and these guys arrive all the time, so what can we do?

Finally, they had to close down. She looked exhausted and he was suffering from nerves and between the two, it was obvious that it would only be a matter of time before their marriage would suffer. Now he runs a fishing shop. Less money, but a normal life. Anyway, fishing was his greatest passion. It was a shame, shame, shame.

So I'm back for a drink on Saturday and I miss the old place. Poor quality techno music floods the room, but I don't mind that. A dog barks in the corner as two drunks get into a fight. One of them is covered in muck from wherever he snoozed during the day, and the other is pulling on a cigarette while he thumps his drinking companion. Eventually, something happens to distract their attention for a moment and they sit down, forgetting that they were ever fighting in the first place.

This young guy comes up to me and asks me if I want to sit down. I tell him I'd rather stand and he looks a bit disappointed. He sits back down but continues to smile over at me. Up he comes again. Maybe you want a drink, he asks. I'm fine, I tell him. But he persists and finally I give in. I recognise him from around the town and he seems like a nice bloke.

He asks me how things are in England. I tell him I'm not from England and he's baffled. When I tell him I'm from Ireland, his brain goes into a flurry of activity with little light shed at the end of it. It's to the left of England, I tell him. The island. He concentrates on an imaginary map but shakes his head and laughs. 'Doesn't matter,' he says.

I teach his girlfriend. She's doing her 'Matura' exam soon. He asks me about her progress with his eyes twinkling like dew on grass. She's beautiful, he tells me, and I agree. But the truth is I never liked her. She is intelligent but arrogant.

I could also tell him right there and then that as soon as the last bell rings on the last day of school she will be gone from his life. The signs are there. He is mad about her – hanging around the school during the day, peeping in windows, smoking, waiting on the steps for about an hour or two before the final bell rings. Then she comes out and they walk home together. That walk, which probably only lasts about fifteen minutes, is the light at the end of this guy's tunnel.

He wants to marry her, but her parents won't agree. They don't think he's good enough for her, since he only finished technical school, specialising in cookery. Now he works in a pizza restaurant and makes good pizzas. His ambition, he tells me, is to be able to cook for her as a husband. If he married her, she'd never have to do a thing.

By the end of the night he's drunk, raving about the girlfriend, the parents, money and other existential crises. Finally, my young companion insists on escorting me home and promises to phone me for the next disco in the Zajazd, the place where I'd had the teacher's meal but which has also since become a mafia locale. I thank him, assuming that it's the last I'll hear from him.

He does phone me a few weeks later, but I decline. His girlfriend has given him the flick and I don't think he'll handle it too well. God bless him, he is such a genuine and decent bloke. That's his dream over with though, and off he'll go to the army. That guy in Warsaw? He'll avoid the army, because he'll be in college long enough to keep out of it. But I'm still glad that I ended up in Minsk.

There was a particular girl I taught the first year I came over. She was in one of the post-maturity classes. Some of the girls in this group were a lot friendlier outside the school than in it. They were really just bored. I got to know some of them better over the years and watched the majority succumb to a type of despair that eventually seemed to just become a part of their lives. In school they simply sat there at their desks, sighing and moaning, day after day, week after week.

In each class, however, were those who had the will to overcome this hurdle, and this particular girl always made a real effort. She frequented a bar a little way outside the town and was usually there with her boyfriend, older than she was and a terribly nice fellow if a bit of a barfly. Figuring that he would either serve the alcoholics or become one himself, he had bought a bar eventually. They got married, and between the two of them tried to get a life together. After a year, the council closed the bar down, saying that it was selling drugs. But the word around the town was that another bar didn't like having competition so close. Bribes were exchanged and the young couple were put out of business. The last I heard of them, they had moved in with her parents.

I have mentioned the 'Matura' often enough, so it's worth describing briefly what it involves. At the end of each school year, I had to sit on a panel with several other teachers and examine those students who had chosen English as one of their Matura subjects. There are times even now when my conscience haunts me over the whole thing. Year after year, you saw the same few girls do nothing in lessons and less at home, then burst into tears outside the examination room when their grades were dismal. If they failed, they repeated the exam; if they failed again, they repeated the year. The first time round I was very lenient. The second year I was less so, but made sure that no student failed. After that I began to harden up, primarily because I tried to work hard with the students and half of them did diddly squat.

This latter half, I learned, chose English because they figured it was easier than the other subjects available. Or, more likely, I was easier than the teachers that taught those other subjects. So I decided eventually that I was going to fail a few to change that view.

I remember one girl who could barely put a sentence together in English. When she did manage a bunch of words, it barely made sense. If it did make sense, it was the wrong answer anyway. The other two English teachers carried on regardless, smiling when the girl had finished. She was a nice girl, friendly, polite and good-natured, but did nothing in class except have a giggle and a chat, winking at me every now and again if I told her off.

During the exam, which might take anything from three to eight hours depending on the number of students present, food is brought in, along with tea, minerals and cakes, by a chosen team of parents whose daughters are sitting that subject. They hang around outside the door, glancing in at every opportunity and rushing to refill your cup. It is a nice gesture and very typical of Polish society. However, at the end of the exam, when we were conferring, I had this particular girl down for a

'2' grade – a borderline pass technically, but regarded by most as a fail.

The teacher beside me, however, had her down for a '4', which is an honour. When I went to protest, I was given a sharp kick on the ankle under the table and told to shut up, as her mother had made the tea and cakes. Meanwhile, girls who I knew had worked their arses off but may not have performed brilliantly on the day, received a '3' grade, which is a straight pass.

It was a total joke. I had several rows about it afterwards, but, although the other teachers knew I was right, they felt there was nothing they could do about it. The same problem applied across the board. I had colleagues in other schools who had been visited by distraught parents in the middle of the night with bottles of vodka and money. It was a mess, but it was a mess that had always been there. How were kids supposed to come out of a system like that?

Thereafter, I decided to be as corrupt as everyone else, only I let favouritism creep in. If I liked the girl, I would ask an easy question, shaking my head or kicking her under the table if she began heading in the wrong direction. If a girl had given me a hard time all year, I'd throw a stickler at her. I would make it so hard that even if her mother had made the cake to beat all cakes, it would have been impossible to give her a good grade. I didn't do it too often, because really I was too soft and should probably never even have been a teacher.

In the end I couldn't stick it. The last straw was giving two excellent girls a '3' grade pass because they hadn't done well on the day, even though they were brilliant students. I'm not even sure why I gave them a poor mark. Maybe I was just confused with the whole system. But their faces when the results were called out at the end of the day will haunt me forever. In fact, I could barely look them in the eye. When I did, I saw that they were not only shocked at their grades, but deeply disappointed with me for giving them. It was the last exam I ever did.

Thankfully, the Department of Education introduced set exams when I left, with a representative sitting on the panel. Still, there's a danger that the tea and cakes will remain. All Poles love tea and cakes.

Over sixty percent of Polish people don't read books and fifty-eight percent only have two books in the house. This was the finding of a study done at the end of 1999, when the world was on the brink of the new millennium and everyone figured a new era would be ushered in. If the parents don't read, then neither will the kids. I wondered, though, about that statistic. Where was it taken from? Which region? I decided to do my own little survey. When I asked the kids in school how many of them read on a daily basis, I didn't need to actually count the hands. The number was instantly obvious. But if I had asked the rich kids in Warsaw the same question, I guarantee that, despite their party image, the answer would have been very different.

Corporal punishment is strictly forbidden in Polish schools. But I came close to thumping the heads off one particular bunch of kids. I threw them out one morning and missed one of them by mere inches with a large bag that had been left behind. It was one of the few occasions where I actually lost my temper, but it had been boiling for months.

Monday morning they were in, screaming and laughing and swearing in Polish. They never did a thing in lessons and I'm sure it was them that planted that note under the door. The one about breaking my legs or something. I'm also sure it was them firing stones at the window on a regular basis. I got revenge by giving them atrocious marks. Then I began chatting to them a bit more and I think they gave me a bit of respect eventually. But I wanted them to suffer and thought about requesting to have them demoted – keeping them back a year. When I spoke to one of the other English teachers, she appeared troubled by this idea. Two of them were orphans and another guy's parents were divorced, so I was asked to go easy. I made more of an effort with them, not that it paid off. At the end of the year their grades in their Matura wouldn't have got them far. So off they go to the army.

Every young man leaving school is obliged to serve twelve months in the army. This has been the case since 1949, and in 1967 the age for mandatory service was set at nineteen. The basic term was set at two years. The first post-communist regime made some changes however, shortening the term to eighteen months and eventually to just twelve. It will soon be phased out altogether. There are ways of dodging conscription, or there is a choice of spreading it out in short terms over a longer period. But why would you wish to drag out what is viewed by most as a prison term?

The system has four categories: A, B, D and E. A means you're fit and able to serve; B means you're a third-level student and can defer; D means you're medically unfit, but can be called up for active service; E means you're insane and therefore exempt.

The army is a nightmare for the young kids, who join very soon after finishing school. The majority will do whatever it takes to dodge it, although some, of course, go voluntarily for a long term. That way, you at least get to choose your location and regiment. I spoke to two young guys who were in their final year in school. One had no false hopes that he was going on to college, and had resigned himself to the fact that in a few months' time he'd be cowering under a bunk bed trying to escape a barrage of boots. He wasn't great at English, but he was a good kid and worked hard. The other kid was happy to be joining the army. He was volunteering, looking forward to a long career, and felt that it was every young man's patriotic duty to serve for a minimum term. To encourage him, he had a father who was a high-ranking officer.

The punishing of new recruits is a mechanism intrinsic to the very workings of the army. Everyone knows about it, from the officers to the raw recruits, to the mothers who receive letters from kids unable to tolerate the strain. The methods don't look so severe on paper – punches, kickings, dragging recruits through the muck, making them smell dirty clothes, stealing food packages sent from home – but it is abrasive and effective, and eventually the weaker ones fold up. Most soldiers will adopt a recruit as their 'cat' when they enter – a bit like the prison system where a new guy will have to become someone's 'bitch' for his own protection. These 'cats' will inflict the afore-mentioned hardships and personally assist their masters. Some commit suicide. The ones who get out when their time is done could swing any way. They could be mentally unstable; they could be seeking vengeance wherever they can find it; they could become part of the criminal gang system.

If you're rich or lucky enough to get a third-level place, that's one way out. You don't see many of those privileged Warsaw kids in the army. If you're not rich or intelligent, you could fake a medical. This means you're put down as Category D or E and it's stamped in your ID, which all future prospective employers will wish to see. Those poor guys, the ones with no grades, they'll get their year in the army all right. But what will it prepare them for?

The Good Thief

At this stage, 1999 and my fourth year, I had become what you might call an expatriate, although I don't very much like that term. It suggests Brits over in India with gins and tonics, mixing homogeneously and dreaming of England.

I prefer something like a 'comfortable misfit', as I was fitting in perfectly well, despite being a foreigner, and wasn't dreaming about home as much as I used to. It is an odd feeling, immersing yourself in another culture. You grow comfortable enough with the language. You settle into your job and accept it for what it is. You also assimilate the habits of the locals – eating as they do, drinking as they do, swearing and cursing as they do, supporting the local football team and turning your nose up at Guinness in favour of the local brew when you visit trendy bars in bigger cities. To a point, of course.

Supporting their football team was something that the locals were surprised at one day. It was a World Cup qualifier between England and Poland, and the match was only on satellite television.

Satellite television was still a rare enough phenomenon, and few would have been able to watch the match.

So the council stepped in and decided to screen it in the town cultural building for a small fee. Needless to say, the place was mobbed. Whole families turned up in the park outside hours beforehand with packed lunches, vodka and those big sausages, all ready for a grand day out.

Myself and my pal Paul, also still in the country, managed to find a small, dingy bar that was showing the match. It was also mobbed, but at least it was a bar rather than a large hall. The few hostile leers turned to confusion when England scored and we began swearing in Polish. Even people I knew quite well couldn't understand it. It was an English victory in the end and any chance of us getting thumped evaporated once they realised – if never quite fully understood – that we were as despondent as them about it.

We had both, in a sense, become attached to the country. Paul was engaged at that point and I was not very far away from it myself. I put it off until my fifth year, when we went into Warsaw one evening, Asha and I, to turn out my pockets and see what sort of ring a spendthrift on €150 a month could afford. It didn't really matter to us at the time what the ring looked like – a homemade job actually. We weren't material as individuals as there wasn't much chance of that on our salaries. The ring only sealed what we knew from the first year was inevitable. There was no question of it ever being otherwise, and it was that knowledge that had kept me in Minsk, when otherwise I would have packed up and gone home.

Of course, when you become absorbed in another culture to such a degree, you become aware of its negative aspects also. One of these aspects is crime, something that everyone, no matter where they go, has to be aware of. Luckily, I never got too close to being a victim.

The trains that I mentioned earlier are a nightmare when you're coming home late. Stories like this one abound. It was the last train from Warsaw, 12.30 at night, and this young guy was coming home to Minsk, about an hour's journey. Two louts approached him and demanded his money. He foolishly pulled a canister of CS gas and began spraying them like flies.

CS gas is not the best thing in the world to pull on these people. I bought a can myself, but eventually decided to leave it at home. Firstly, if the coppers catch you with it you're in trouble. It is illegal for a member of the public to possess it, but in Warsaw, you can buy anything. The biggest open-air market in the world is in Warsaw's Stadion (Stadium) – everything from guns, gas, old Russian cameras, pirate CDs and videos, to prostitutes doing the job on-location can be found there. Traders come from everywhere – though mostly from Russia – and with them come the travelling brothels. It's a disturbing place, because of its sheer size and the number of dodgy-looking characters creeping around it. Muggings are rife. It is also brilliant for its chaos and diversity – you could literally spend days browsing. And if you dress down, nobody will bother you. Sadly, it was also being earmarked for development.

Secondly, if you spray one of these thugs with gas, you had better make sure you spray them good. Into the eyes first time and be ready to run like a scalded cat. CS gas is not pleasant, and if you don't do it right and give yourself a chance to flee then it's like stirring a hornet's nest. Also, sometimes you might buy something called 'CS gas', but find that it is actually only pepper spray, used to give dogs a bit of a fright. You'll really get the guys going with that one, and they'll thump you round the train like a pork chop because of it.

Anyway, how far can you run on a train doing eighty miles an hour? Where are you going to go? Don't expect other passengers – if there are any – to help you. They just run into the next compartment and hide under the seats at the slightest sign of trouble.

So this young guy did exactly what he shouldn't have done. Worse still, there were two more thugs he hadn't seen in the next compartment. They didn't like the CS gas either. So, after beating him half unconscious, they dragged him to the doorway, opened the doors and flung him out onto the tracks. Miraculously, he survived. I imagine he was lucky enough to land on the far bank, or maybe the train was slowing down as it approached a station. The story around the town was that he was an off-duty cop who got too brave.

Another man, a teacher who had worked in my school, had recently died after several years bedridden from a similar incident on a train. I had never met him, but knew his daughter. He was an exceptionally popular man and prayers were always said for his recovery whenever there was a teachers' get-together. Sadly, he didn't make it.

The money is nothing, give it to them. And if you have to take a few digs, okay, sit there, close your eyes and hope it won't last too long.

I got that last train regularly and dreaded the trip. It comes rattling out of the tunnel like a great iron horse, dark and intimidating, sometimes with several of the windows and lights smashed in the rear compartments. You have to go for the front because of the ghouls that hang around at the back, but even then you've no guarantee. As people get off and carriages empty, you run up and down looking for other passengers to make you feel safer. But who do you feel safe with at one o'clock in the morning?

One night I was coming home from Warsaw after spending the Friday evening in a pub after work with a mate of mine. We'd drank a good few beers and as each hour passed I knew I was pushing it close to the last train. So I left, pretty drunk and very tired, and got the 11.30 train, which is almost as bad. The carriage was fairly empty apart from one or two other drunkards asleep on the seats and it wasn't long before I fell asleep with them. It was always a good idea to blend in with the drunkards on these late trains to avoid becoming a target. So I'd always try and be half drunk anyway, sipping on a can of beer and pressing my head against the window looking destitute. I had with me my equipment I used in the radio station for interviews and my small green rucksack, which has gone everywhere with me for years.

When the train pulled into Minsk, I woke up and got off in a hurry, leaving the green bag behind. Halfway down the road I realised what I'd done and almost cried. In it were a few cans of beer, three or four books I'd bought, a range of discs with months of work on them and two videos from the British Council library. The British Council is a life-saving institution that has centres all over the world. Each centre not only runs courses in English but contains a library with books, videos and tapes. If you lose them though, you'll obviously have to pay. But the money doesn't always compensate, since a lot of the films they have are old and irreplaceable.

The next day I asked around as to the whereabouts of the lost property office in Siedlce, which is the terminus for the local trains. The Polish friends thought this was great gas. Lost property? If it's lost then it's no longer your property. The chances were the bag was stolen and thrown in a ditch somewhere, or if it was found by a conductor or cleaner it was rifled and was now lying lonely and empty on the track.

The next day, Sunday, saw a blizzard that would have stopped a war. After ruminating all afternoon I ventured out late in the evening to Siedlce, where I was told a lost property office of sorts existed on one of the platforms. People said I was mad. But through some bewildering twist of fate, my bag was there and was returned by a kind old woman, with a not-so-kind young man in the back of the office breaking into fits of laughter. My discs are there; so too are the magazines. The beer, the books, my glasses and the videos – Father Ted and a Dudley Moore & Cook comedy – are gone. Anything that can be drunk, eaten or sold will be taken. You have to remember that. So someone, somewhere, that weekend, was watching my Father Ted, through my glasses, and drinking my beer. I hope they enjoyed it. Because I never got to, having to foot the bill instead. But the baffling thing was, whoever stole the bag had the decency to hand it into the lost property office. A thief with a conscience.

Crime, unfortunately, was a subject that was very difficult to avoid. People were obsessed with it. Equally depressing were constant reminders that, although Poland was not exactly the safest place to be, at least you could be comforted with the statistic that eighty percent of crimes were urban. There was a programme on Polish television, something similar to the 'Crimewatch' programmes, designed to aid police, only the Polish show was like the triple-X certificate version of the ones shown on RTÉ or the BBC.

Where reconstructions of crimes would normally leave something to the imagination, the Poles evidently decided at some stage that the shock factor would be more effective for jogging people's memories. You get vivid portrayals of young girls being kidnapped from villages and driven off into the woods in the backs of vans. Women knocked unconscious, raped and set on fire during break-ins. Gangs tearing around, having a ball, kicking in heads. This programme also had a curious habit of showing horrendous pictures of the victims, as if the reconstructions weren't harrowing enough.

I remember talking about this with some of my Polish friends. They simply shook their heads and told me, for God's sake, to stop watching it. That was hard though. It seemed to be the most popular programme on television and was repeated several times a week. I didn't dwell on it too much, but there seemed to be a lot of negative energy floating around this country that needed a focal point. But there wasn't one.

On Polish radio, a professional car thief said that stealing cars was his job. He had to make a living like everybody else. No bother to him. I know there are groups of guys in Warsaw who will gladly 'sort out' a problem for a few bottles of vodka. And I wouldn't like to be 'sorted out' by these fellas. One of my colleagues was attacked in the park in Warsaw by a gang of about five men, armed with iron bars, knuckle-dusters and baseball bats. He made the mistake of going through the park after visiting the Irish bar. But it takes about half an hour off the route to the train station. I've done it myself hundreds of times. You have a few drinks, take a look into the park and decide, 'To hell with it. I'll risk it.' These thugs wanted money and they made sure they were going to get a kick out of getting it.

That's the more disturbing aspect. You can part with your money, but picking up your front teeth is a whole different thing. This guy was lucky. He's big and fit and came away with his life. I wouldn't have made it.

A sixteen-year-old girl from my school was pulled into the woods here and raped in broad daylight by three guys who were all drunk on vodka. They then beat her and left her unconscious in the hopes that she wouldn't remember who did it. That's what they told the police. I could go on, but why bother? It's not my intention to make Poland look bad, and crime exists everywhere. But it leads me back to all of the negative energy floating around in this country. And crime, as somebody said, is simply misguided energy.

It is after midnight in the newly paved square in Minsk. They've done a great job here, transforming a patch of grass in the centre into a cobblelock plaza – it's hardly Milan, but it's a pleasant place to sit on a summer evening. I recall my first year here, when the pavements were all collapsing into the sand. Now there has been a transformation. The proprietor of the local cinema directly opposite the square has taken full advantage and opened a bar on the pavement. Genius. Now we've somewhere to sit and have a beer in the summer.

A white BMW cruises past, humming like a large wasp. The BMWs here belong either to those who have worked their arses off to get the money, or those who have stolen it from them.

The beamer slows as it passes me and, like a lazy animal opening one eye after a doze, rolls down a window to get a closer look. Two muggish-looking faces peer out at me – one with his lip curled up in the corner in a sneer of contempt, a vain effort at a moustache sprinkled across the top. He must be about seventeen and looks like a 'Gypsy', as Poles call them. The Gypsies here are mostly Roma, and a lot of them have settled down and become quite well-off with stalls on the markets.

One of these Gypsies wanted to do me in once, the boyfriend of a student of mine. She was a nice wee girl who then turned into a right little cow, so I gave her bad grades. He wanted revenge for that. Somebody, somewhere, intervened on my behalf, telling him that if anything happened to me, he was dead. For a while though, it looked as if I was in trouble. Stones at my window and long stares in the pub. It upset me for a while and didn't help my sleeping patterns.

The beamer follows me for a few yards and I get a bit nervous. Then it suddenly takes off, with a screech and a hot blast of burning rubber. I let out a sigh of relief and cross the square. It's quite pretty, but those benches – although transforming the appearance of a once drab-looking street – will do nothing but attract the mobs. And here they are.

As I walk past, one of the mob, with a baseball cap on back-to-front, leaps off the bench and lands in a pose, punching the air, then kicking over his head like an excited ballerina. 'C'mon!' he screams, beating his fists off his singlet-covered chest. 'C'mon!' he shouts again. He even has an American accent, so either he has an American teacher, or he's been watching too much Gangsta TV.

Meanwhile, just as I reach the far side and turn off into a side street, a large police van enters the square. It passes the BMW that had hung over me like a vulture, passes even the benches with the mobs, the spit and the broken bottles. Passes the singlet-clad gangsta rappa guy, who's still leaping around like a monkey. Then, of all things, it pulls in front of me and blocks my path. The window goes down and two serious-looking coppers with moustaches glare out of the window.

'ID,' one says, with a stern voice.

I have only had a few jars all night. I'm walking perfectly straight and am dressed in a pair of jeans and a T-shirt. I'm about as suspicious as a fish on Good Friday, yet they pull me up and demand I identify myself. I actually smile with the absurdity of it and, turning to point at the mobs on the benches drinking – which has become illegal on the streets of Poland – ask them if I have done something wrong.

Now, the cops here are pretty unpopular. Most of them spend their time trying to catch poor innocent folk at petty crime, because they know they'll get a handover. Cross the road without a green man and they'll stop you and demand a 'fine'. They stop cars all over the place, telling them they were speeding and must go to the station.

Nobody wants to go to the station, so they pay thirty or forty zlotys instead.

I was locked out of my flat one night, because the hall in the building was being used for a wedding. The 'security guard' was an off-duty copper and he kicked the crap out of a friend and I when we tried to force our way in. He thought we were Russians, he said. Nothing was done. Two policemen in plain clothes visited me and asked various questions, but because I wasn't black and blue all over they didn't seem too concerned. Also, we'd had a few drinks. Once the police hear there is drink involved in any incident, they simply shrug their shoulders and walk away.

The cop in the van now pulls out a pen and notebook and starts asking me questions. Where do I live, where was I all evening, and so on. Then he asks for my parents' names and address. I begin to explain that I'm not Polish and he says, 'Just tell me your parents' names and address.' I tell him, then he consults with the other policeman before waving me away. They knew me at this point. Or at least knew of me, after the incident in the boarding block.

In my first year, I was actually put in the van and driven home to prove I wasn't some undesirable scouring the neighbourhood for a good target. I had been walking home with my guitar when they pulled over and jumped out in front of me. I was shocked. Martial law had ended years ago. There was no need to throw people up against walls and demand IDs just because it was after ten o'clock. They opened the case and inspected the guitar, finally putting me into the van as I gave them directions to where I lived. It was Friday night and the boarding block was locked. I opened the door with my key and immediately the woman on duty woke up, running out into the hall to find me with two coppers. One of the policemen went up to her and said, this guy – me – claims to live here.

'Well, of course he does if he has a key! Are you stupid?'

Nobody would have spoken to them like that a few years earlier.

Trying to find out why the police stopped me and not the mobsters, I ask the kids in school. They shrug. This is nothing new, they tell me. It is because the cops are afraid. They're too afraid to hold up the thugs and I was an easier target. They were hoping I was drunk and they'd get a fine or a bribe or something.

A young family I knew were completing the construction of a new house and left it unattended for a few days. When they returned, everything – from the sinks, toilets and pipes to the beams – was gone. Not a washer or spare brick left. The louts who ransacked the place, of course, will accept anything from a couple of bottles of vodka to a few miserable zlotys as a price.

They have a lodger there now, who says he's going to dig a pit in the garden – something similar to a bear trap. His brother, he says, is a doctor, and can give him acid that will dissolve bodies like piss on a snowman. Anyone coming over the fence is a dead man. I'm inclined to believe him. He seems pretty serious about protecting himself. He killed a dog in Warsaw not so long ago. A Rottweiler. The owner stood and laughed as the dog – with no muzzle and let off the leash – charged towards him. He warned the owner to call him back, but was ignored. So he broke the dog's neck in an instant. Perhaps a year in the army might be useful after all.

The Last Waltz

As the level on the thermometer drops, so too does the spirit. Every book has been read and sits exhausted in a clumsy row on a long table, a large jar of water at each end to keep them from collapsing in a heap. I develop the pallor of their pages every year, once the month of October registers on the calendar – a sort of yellowy-white, like an old lightbulb. There isn't enough natural light in this place to grow a weed. Winter chokes the life out of everything.

Despite the number of years that had passed, the Polish winter was something I couldn't get used to. Novelty was replaced by a stale sense of habit, work became tedious and even the students that I once went out with had disappeared, the new ones that bit too young to socialise with. The merits of living alone were growing tiresome and the demerits becoming all too clear. To keep my mind healthy I had to find something to occupy my thoughts.

There was an insignificant little town, a 'burak' town, called Kaluszyn, sitting roughly ten kilometres away from my own on the dismal road that led to the Russian border. A nondescript, functionless ghost town, nothing came through here but buses to somewhere else and few people came out permanently but the dead. There was little that stood out, save a redbrick church that had survived the war and a brand spanking new foreign garage that sold imported beer and Red Bull.

This garage was an oasis in a town that drifted off to sleep some time after five every evening. Little else stirred but the wind sweeping in from the Urals. For heavy drinkers, the hatch that serviced customers nightly must surely have seemed like God's great dumb waiter. Once the tiny hotdog and beer bar near the bus stop – for it wasn't really a station, just a muddy car park and a shelter – closed, the garage was the only thing open.

Not that the town was hideously ugly. It certainly had its charm, as many towns in the eastern part of the country do. It wouldn't be surprising to see them on postcards sold to tourists in Warsaw. But they give off an air of stagnation, impossible not to detect after spending any amount of time there.

The demographics of Kaluszyn were similar to any other rural residential area, with several generations living under one roof in many households. Most of the kids that lived there attended the schools in Minsk, while those who had finished either resigned themselves to permanent unemployment, commuted to work in Warsaw or had gone to cities like Gdansk, Poznan or Lodz for third-level studies.

This last group were the lucky ones. For the males it meant avoiding conscription; for females avoiding the premature band of gold that convention often dictated. I wept annually for the girls in my school who went directly from the exam halls to the church, with a seventeen-year-old kid on their arm who was about to enter the army because he couldn't get an education. Marriage for these girls is a stage of life immediately following puberty. They should really pencil it in to the biology prospectus.

It is hard to imagine life in these towns from a Western perspective. Before we went to Poland, we were given a talk by a Polish teacher who lived in a spot not entirely unlike this one. Shaking her head and looking around at us all, she scowled and said, 'You must understand, there is nothing to do in a lot of towns and villages in Poland. Nothing.'

Of course, that meant little to most of us. A town is a town as far as we were concerned and, unless it's located in the wilderness of Siberia, all towns share the same facilities. But when she said there was nothing to do, she meant there was nothing to do. After five in the evening, a place such as Kaluszyn turned into a ghost town. There was no cinema, although occasionally a film would be shown on a screen erected in the town hall. Even towns with cinemas never guaranteed a screening. The cinema in my town – which at least was a town and not a village – was vital every Sunday. I would head down no matter what the film. But there were many occasions when not enough people turned up – I think it needed a minimum of fifteen. Then the owner would just shrug and the movie wouldn't be shown. The long walk back to the flat on a Sunday night in winter was devastating.

Besides perhaps from a kiosk near the bus shelter and a small, pathetic café, there would be no real bar. Sports facilities? In my school there was an area to kick a ball around. That was it. Imagine in the middle of winter what it must be like to live in one of these villages. For entertainment, people simply call to each other's homes with bottles of vodka. If you are too young to drink, you get someone older to buy a bottle and find a bench, a bus shelter or a group of trees, where you stay until the drink is finished and you begin to feel the cold.

At this point in time, the late 1990s, the rest of Europe was going through the Ecstasy era. Clubs had taken live music venues out of circulation and anyone I knew back in Ireland of my age was out on pills until seven in the morning. I lost a few friends for a while back then, thinking during short trips back home that I would be going out for a few pints with the guys on a night out. Next thing, their shirts are off and they're standing in front of the DJ box with their hands in the air. I didn't get it. That whole scene passed me by. I only ever got to read about it in *Hot Press*, which I subscribed to during my time in Poland. Otherwise, I remained clueless. The isolation was very real.

Whatever about finding pills and clubs in Warsaw, the chances of it in Minsk were slim. Anyway, the bulk of drugs in Poland were homemade, mostly derivatives of heroin in some lethal blend or other. In fact, drug production in Poland began in 1975, when a medical student in Gdansk came up with a drug known as 'kompot', the name of the fruit drink I used to get with lunch in the internat, but obviously not containing the same ingredients. Kompot, or brown sugar as it was also known, was made over a kitchen stove using the husks of poppies that grew in Poland's fields. Apparently, it was three times stronger than heroin in the West. It was highly addictive, and very attractive to a lot of depressed young people from the 1970s onwards. It was also very cheap, and in the 1980s, Warsaw was dubbed 'little Nepal', with addicts in the country numbering over 100,000.

Drugs certainly didn't have the glamour that made them the poison of choice back home in the 1990s. If you were on drugs in Poland, you were a 'narcoman', a depressed, hopeless case, because the drugs were just lethal. In time it would change. But I never knew anyone who was on anything stronger than a bit of dope at the time.

The young people of Kaluszyn, however, had done something for themselves. They had made a club and this club belonged to them – the college students, teenagers and unemployed. They cherished it for all they were worth, since there wasn't one other scrap of property they could meet in. The club was located in the basement of the local primary school, oddly enough. Down where the pipes and furnaces that heated the school were located they had made a bar and a stage. They had got together several couches and a toilet, and there was enough space to fit well over a hundred people. They even had their own sound and lighting equipment. In the winter it was warm, and in the summer you could open up the doors to allow a cool draught sweep through. This was where the kids celebrated New Year's Eve and birthday parties, where they came to chat and mingle on a Saturday night. It was kept safe, clean and free from scumbags, and consequently the parents and police let it be.

One evening I was invited there for a party. I had met a band from this town, who played one night in a new pub that had opened in Minsk – a very welcome addition after three years of cafés. At the time I was playing in pubs in Warsaw, having been a part-time musician for many years. I was enjoying the gigs in Warsaw because it got me out of Minsk, but was tiring of ex-pats screaming for U2 songs on a Saturday night. Anyhow, I was far more interested in playing with a blues band. So I accepted the invitation gladly.

On this particular night, they were having their last party before 'Post'. Post is a religious period of abstinence, in this case coinciding with Lent. As with Christmas, during this period it is forbidden to dance, sing or go to clubs. So for the young people, this was the last great hooley for some time and the majority resented the fact. For them, the last night is something of a wake. When it is all over, it's as if you've turned their humour off with a switch. Yet, bizarrely enough, they abide by the rules, which have been set down by the Church.

I had a St Patrick's Day party in this club a few weeks later and not one soul got up off their chair except to visit the toilet. At the end of the night when I put on the Pogues, one young guy went berserk, throwing caution to the wind and dancing around like a clown. But he got a serious reprimand from his peers, and no doubt spent the following afternoon in the confession box. It is a very, very strange thing to watch people in the prime of their youth behaving in such a way; even they couldn't really explain it to me.

'It's post, Tom. We can't dance,' they'd say with a shrug, before gulping down a quick contraband beer or vodka with a grimace. 'But it will be over soon.' What they couldn't figure out was how I, as a Catholic, didn't have to adhere by the same rules. I couldn't explain to them why the rules for Irish Catholics are different than those for Polish Catholics.

Poland is renowned for having some of the finest musicians in the world, with jazz and classical music being the most prominent musical forms. That night in their club, there were guys present who were top musicians in full-time jazz academies in Warsaw. They needed a place to play and this was it, a basement club under a school, the type of club a slightly older Famous Five might construct. The music, however, was like something from the pages of Kerouac. And the fact that there was nobody there of any note to witness it added a certain ephemeral glory to the whole occasion. One by one, musicians took to the stage, backed by the group that I had previously met and who could literally turn their hand to any style. If there was ever a point where I predicted a future for a group of individuals, it was here.

I had yet to come across people with such energy, commitment and talent, and was firmly convinced that within a year or two this tale would have a happy ending. Unfortunately, it all ended very sadly indeed. And I tend to look at what happened with that band as a sort of case study of youth in such circumstances in Poland.

Apart from one member, who was actually a student of mine, they were all in their early to mid-twenties. The band was led by a guy called Jarek, a sensational guitar player who at the time was waiting for a place to turn up in a college somewhere. He was ambitious, perhaps the most ambitious of the group, and above all had his sights firmly set on the road that led out of town. He was also quite moody, swinging between a cheerful but composed temper and a cantankerous one. I admit in the beginning being unsure about the guy, although that sentiment didn't last, and in fact he became a good friend. He was simply a very motivated young man, very aware that life outside the confines of the town he grew up in had a lot more to offer, if only he got a chance.

Jarek's cousin Pawel, who played bass, was the band's eldest member. He had worked as a hairdresser all his life until he quit and began working in a factory that, from what I could gather, had something to do with upholstery.

He never wished to talk about what he did. Nobody else in the band really seemed to know either. To supplement his small income, he played in a 'wedding' band during the wedding season. It seemed he hated this as much as he hated his day job, but it paid well.

Wedding season is generally in the summer. People get married in droves, with churches churning out one wedding after the other on a Saturday. The parties begin in the late afternoon and continue until sunrise the following morning, most continuing for a day or two afterwards. The music is provided by a wedding band playing Polish folk and that appalling Disco Polo I spoke of earlier. I grew very familiar with weddings. Marriage was a constant topic for many of the girls in school, and the dining area in the internat was also rented out for wedding receptions during the summer. Having one of those bands beneath your room every Saturday night from dusk until dawn, May to September, is perhaps the worst of my memories that has yet to leave me. But at least I never had to play with them.

Pawel was an instantly likeable chap, though again, he was possessed of moods that swung like a pendulum. He would either greet you with a wide grin and a warm handshake or simply not greet you at all. I soon discovered that, in general, his good moods and warm greetings were accompanied with drink of some sort and his bad moods with a hangover. When he had a wedding he drank like a hoor, the vodka and food being part of the contract. And, believe me, it was not unlike these guys to put away two bottles each over the course of a long night. The next day at rehearsals, he'd be like a bull.

The drummer was a guy called Kazik, the diminutive of Kazikowski, his surname. When I first met him, he was a vibrant, exceptionally friendly young man in his mid-twenties, who was looking to get work in the IT sector. However, when his girlfriend split up with him he literally disappeared – he was found in a hospital about a month later after a marathon drinking binge. At the time, I couldn't comprehend it. I could comprehend even less the attitude of the rest of the band members, who simply dismissed the whole episode with no explanation and a brush of the hand. In time, I learned that such binging was, if not necessarily accepted, at least tolerated. I must admit that, witnessing more and more of the same myself, I eventually grew as impervious to it as everyone else.

When Kazik finally returned he had his hair cut, his girl-friend and his demeanour back, and not a word was said on the matter. It was as if he had never left at all.

The final member of the band was the younger Pawel, who attended the art section in my school and was some-times the butt of the group's jokes. A quiet lad of only about seventeen, he was left at the back of the stage as rhythm guitarist, receiving scowls from Jarek at regular intervals if his playing lapsed. I didn't see him lasting long in the band and was actually happy for him because of it. He was a talented artist, who only needed a bit more enthusiasm and encouragement to set him on a path to a decent career. He finally got that and went off to university some time later.

After a couple of months, the band asked me to join them as singer/harmonica player, to play rhythm and blues. I was delighted, for many reasons – primarily because I was sick to death of playing in the ex-pat pubs in Warsaw, but also because I was stagnating in Minsk, with no hobbies besides reading and binging.

As a band, the will to work was there. Unfortunately, it just wasn't always there at the same time. We rehearsed on Sundays, which was a bad day to do anything. Sundays in Poland are days of rest. And I mean, days of rest. Most Poles won't lift a finger on Sundays. Whole towns go into shutdown mode. If you want to get anything, you generally have to get it by one o'clock or you starve. Although I usually managed to pick up a cooked chicken from a kiosk that remained open a bit longer at the train station.

I had to travel to Kalusyn every week, with the cooked chicken under my arm, which was a bit of a chore for me. In winter on Sunday, when you're tired and feeling miserable, the last thing you want to do is to sit on the cold back seat of a bus. My general Sunday routine was to stay in bed for most of it, getting up when the greater part of the day was gone, head to the cinema and then go back to bed until Monday.

Rehearsals generally started at around three, which meant I didn't get up until about one. It was dark and cold when I left, dark and freezing when I returned home. No breakfast, no dinner, just coffee or beer and the chicken at the clubhouse, with the musty odour of cigarettes and dirty guitar strings.

We would all arrive on a Sunday afternoon carrying various moods with us. Pawel the bass player was the most unpredictable. It depended on how much vodka he had drunk on Saturday, and how much he wanted to drink on Sunday. Many times I'd arrive at the club and he'd be asleep on the couch. No one would wake him until we were all plugged in and ready to go. Kazik was always willing to work when he was able, but the problem there was getting him to sit behind his kit for long enough to get through a decent set. He was a bit of a drinker too, and he'd be up off his seat every ten minutes for either a beer, a cigarette or a visit to the toilet. It drove Jarek mad, but I just found it amusing.

With rehearsals going as well as could be expected, the next problem facing us was our name. They had been called 'After All' until I came along and disregarded it. It wasn't bluesy enough and didn't have any ring to it. I proposed 'Comfortably Southern' and 'Blue Juice', and we all finally agreed with the former. A week later at rehearsals, they came up to me with long faces. None of the Poles could pronounce it. So we went back to the drawing board and a monosyllabic title that I don't even want to remember was finally decided upon.

It was some six months later when our first gig proper

was organised. Before that we'd run a few open house parties at the club by way of rehearsal. We had worked hard and had a great sound and it had become really enjoyable. It takes a lot to get two hours of material together and not one of the boys would let up until every number was perfect. Whereas I practised with them every Sunday, they played together every night. That's how dedicated they were.

On the day of the gig I remember being nervous. It was mid-summer and the heat was reminiscent of the day I had first arrived in Poland. We were booked to play in a small bar in Minsk, one that had not been open for very long and was keen to establish itself as something more than just another drinking den for winos.

Most people came out of curiosity, people of all ages. Live music was a very rare thing and it was a grand night out. We won that night and, even though it was a dingy pub in a dingy town way off in the eastern recesses of Poland, it felt good. Because it's the achievement, damn it, albeit short-lived, that makes it worthwhile.

There were many more gigs after the summer, further afield in oddball towns. There were long drives home at night in the backs of vans, with bottles of vodka passed around to keep out the cold. I enjoyed the whole idea of it. It was a good way of letting off steam after a heavy week. We got into a studio and things got better. There was more interest in us as a band. Then the gear got upgraded and a few leaps were made on the ladder, up from the mud-coated rungs at the bottom towards the painted ones at the top. Less crowded but harder work. I remembered, though, what a full-time musician had once said to me: Music is great as a hobby, but not for keeping the fridge full. And the reason for that is simple – the fun goes out of it.

Not everything should be fun, but it helps. I had a little desk calendar in my room that had a new proverb for each day. One sticks in my mind: 'When a man finds what he likes doing and gets paid for it, then he's found his job.' Of course, it's practically impossible to achieve that, and gets harder as time goes on and you're still trying to figure out what it is that will fulfil that wish. But it's a nice goal to work towards.

We were enjoying the band, but we weren't getting paid much. I didn't worry too much about that, I wasn't doing it for money. But some of the guys surely were. Maybe that was one factor that contributed to the rising damp that finally set in, but eventually the fun part began to suffer. Climbing into a cold van on a Tuesday night in the middle of winter to get to a gig when you'd rather be at home with a hot pot of tea is perhaps the best way of having a bad time when you're in a band. The arc of the mood pendulum is wider and people get irritable. After the gig, when the adrenaline is high, it's better. But there's a lot of drinking to carry it forward and a blind man can see that a happy medium is a very difficult thing to find.

There was one gig in a town further south on a Monday evening. A town further south called Sokolow Podlaski, a place really not worth describing. Nobody knew how the hell a gig had been arranged for a Monday evening, but it was, and we had to do it. Kazik was drinking along the way and, as usual, the van was being stopped every twenty minutes for him to get out for a piss in the snow. It was bitterly cold, we were all very miserable, and Pawel the elder was getting annoyed. He had just come from work in the factory and hadn't eaten and all he wanted to do was get the whole thing over with and head home to bed.

When we arrived, the place was inert and empty. All the gear had to be carried down into the club from the cold car park. Pawel and I went off to find some food, managing to get two microwave hamburgers each from one of those hotdog kiosks. I normally wouldn't go near them, but we had no alternative. Standing outside in the stiff evening with our hands freezing up rapidly, wolfing down the burgers before the sound check, Pawel suddenly tells me with utter sincerity that he's not in the mood and he is either going to be brilliant or a downright disgrace. Either way, he doesn't particularly care.

I think that's what finished it. It didn't look like it at the time, since we had our first gig in Warsaw lined up for the following week. But the jaded expression on his face said it all. There he was, heading towards his thirtieth birthday, eating microwave hamburgers on a freezing Monday night, having just come from his factory job.

I think back now and recall an omen. There was a man who was sort of an adopted member of the band, who came to all the gigs and all the rehearsals without fail. Because the club belonged to the kids in the town, a lot of people would drift in and out on a Sunday and listen to the band. But this man was there every week, at times whispering a few words to Jarek about the sound or the set-up or the quality of new numbers. Apart from that he rarely spoke. He just sat, listened and drank. He was probably in his forties, but looked a hell of a lot older because he was a bit of a boozer. I only ever knew him by his first name, Janusz, and whenever I asked who he was I was simply told that he was an 'old blues man'. I had no idea what that meant, but, used to the guys' reserve, I left it alone. Janusz clearly loved the lads.

One night, however, we played in a bar that had a piano, and at the end of the night when the place was clearing out and we were all sitting around having a beer, Janusz strolled up to the keys and began playing. I can't remember what he played, but whatever it was it was beautiful. It was only then that the guys told me he'd been a professional musician.

The following Saturday, I'm on the bus heading to the club before the gig in Warsaw. The weather is simply fierce. There's a blizzard blowing outside and the driver is crawling along at a snail's pace. Not far out of town the bus stops and I see Kazik getting on. He gives me a wave and as he pushes through the people to get to the back to where I'm sitting, I notice something unusual about him. He's pissed, but that's not wholly unusual. This time he resembles a soulless carcass. He looks like he hasn't slept in two days and as he sits down and begins to explain things to me, it turns out that it's exactly that.

Today is Saturday. Himself and Pawel the elder were out on Thursday, watching some local band in the pub in Minsk. They are both fairly heavy drinkers, but the amount consumed that evening must have been double the normal and an argument ensued. Kazik got called a crap drummer and Pawel got called a crap bass player. As a result of this simple trade of words, Kazik became depressed and continued on the binge through Friday, Friday night, Saturday morning and this afternoon.

'Tom,' he says, as his pickled eyes roll over in their sockets, 'this is our last concert.'

He can barely keep his head up and when we get off the bus, I have to carry him through the driving snow to the club, where the younger Pawel and Jarek sit waiting. As soon as Jarek sees the two of us approaching, his face literally caves in. His patience had been waning anyway over the past few weeks, with the amount of drinking at rehearsals and the unprofessional approach towards the band as a whole. There had been arguments, which I kept out of. I was only ever there once a week, and stayed away from the jar on most occasions. From what I could see, whatever the problem was, it went back years. The drinking was more deep-rooted and there was nothing I could do about it.

Kazik is placed on the couch and quickly regresses into the land of nod. I try to do the explaining, but it's not easy. Young Pawel simply looks inconsolable and my heart goes out to him. At only seventeen, he probably viewed all this as a possible break and had sat in his room with his guitar on his lap for five hours a day. Jarek doesn't even look at me while I talk. He simply shakes his head and stares at the sleeping Kazik, who shows no signs of waking up, never mind being able to clench a pair of drumsticks.

'So, where's Pawel?' Jarek suddenly asks. Nobody knows. So we wait. Finally, after half an hour under the most taut ceiling of silence, Jarek swears and goes out to phone him. Although I think his condition is rather obvious to all by now.

Ten minutes later, Jarek bursts back in, telling me to ring the bar in Warsaw and cancel the gig. It seems that Pawel did exactly the same thing as Kazik and is now in bed, somewhere away down the yellow brick road with a bottle of vodka.

It may be difficult for people back home to appreciate the role alcohol plays in Poland. For us, we go out on a Friday or Saturday, over-indulge a bit and get our act together again for work on Monday. We're aware of what we're doing and we know it has to come to an end. For a lot of Poles, used to dissatisfaction in many areas of life, that end is not perceived. If they start on a binge, it doesn't matter if it goes on for days. If it puts them in a happier state of mind, they'll stay there until they feel it's time to cope with whatever it is they've run away from. If they don't turn up for work, so be it. So, when Jarek tells me to cancel the gig, he knows what he is talking about. These guys could be out for the next week. Unfortunately, though, it isn't that simple.

The venue, Morgan's Irish Bar, is a popular Irish bar run by a man from Northern Ireland, Ollie, who has always been really decent to me and other fellow travellers. He has put people up in his own house when they were stuck, and gives everyone credit behind the bar. He was the first Irishman I met in Warsaw and he made us all feel like a group of close friends. I played the odd gig in his first bar, sometimes sitting there to wait for the first train back to Minsk at 5am. Ollie would still be there, telling me to go into the kitchen to make myself a sandwich.

He had opened a far superior bar in the centre of Warsaw and was booking in bands to attract the crowds. I just couldn't afford to leave him without a band on a Saturday night.

So I go over to where Pawel lives and after arguing with his mother, manage to root him out of bed. He emerges finally, half dressed and laughing like a donkey in the freezing snow and darkness. When we get back to the club, Kazik is being fed with coffee, even though he hasn't woken up yet. Everybody ignores Pawel, who doesn't seem too concerned, searching under the seats for something to drink. Miraculously, we get everyone into the van and on the road to Warsaw. Kazik still hasn't woken up though, and Pawel has managed to find a beer somewhere to get stuck into along the way.

It's a nightmare, it really is. In an hour's time we have to do a two-hour set in a very popular spot. We arrive at around seven to set up, and I inform Ollie that he needn't worry, they're just a bit tired. Right at that moment, Pawel staggers to the bar and orders two-ounce shots of vodka for himself and Kazik, who has finally woken up. Ollie stares. Isn't he one of yours?

The night went well. In fact, it was the best gig we ever did. On the way home in the van, I made a vague attempt at patching up the members of the group. I was going home for Christmas and said we'd all have a nice break and get it together after the holidays. They didn't look convinced. At least, nobody was going to make the first move of reconciliation. A simple handshake was all it would have taken. And I thought the Irish were stubborn.

When I came back after Christmas, there was worse news. The town council had decided to close down the clubhouse. So even if the band were still together, we had no place to rehearse in. It was attracting the wrong people, was the reason given. I wasn't so sure.

'It's a sad day, Tom. A sad day,' is what they said on the evening of the last party, and they were right. The reason may be difficult to grasp for people living and growing up in a Western society, where entertainment and facilities are so readily available the only problem is choice.

But in towns and villages in eastern Poland you don't have a choice. Boredom is as much a part of daily existence as washing, cooking and eating. In between these rites are long, interminable gaps of prolonged tedium, where the mind simply smoulders or descends into apathy. Think of every convenience in your life and try and picture its opposite: in place of your multi-channel television back home, here you get a three-channel vacuum, mostly dedicated to repeats, Brazilian soaps and endless political debates and discussions about the price of pork.

Picture a restaurant with a menu bursting at the sides and replace it with a hot-dog stall, open from ten to six. Picture a pub with a lively unisex clientele and warm music and put in its place a 'drink bar' with ageing alcoholics and slippery bottles of vodka coated with grease. Your multiplex cinema becomes a screen in a cold hall with maybe one film a week, which doesn't run if enough people don't show up. Then you have a few grocery stores, a butcher, maybe a bookshop, and a bus or train to take you the hell out of there a few times a day. That's a small town or village in eastern Poland. It's changing slowly, of course it is. But at that time there was simply nothing.

Even that last party was a flop. I arrived late and missed my turn with the band and people were annoyed with me for it. The club had been cleared out, so it was supposed to be an outdoor party, but the weather didn't cooperate. And as the rain came down, there was more than a touch of irony to add to the occasion. That very same night, the only other 'bar' in the whole place was burned to the ground. Nobody knows what happened, and the bar was a hole anyway – it was really just a little prefab on the side of the road where you could buy cheap bottles of beer and soggy hotdogs. But it was an alternative to a bus shelter or a park bench.

As the people on their way home that night watched their only other alternative crumble into a pile of dying embers, I imagine they knew the taste of irony. Hard, grainy and sour, it probably lingered on a dry tongue for months. The guy I was walking with back to the bus shelter started laughing when he saw the charred carcass.

So there it all came to an end. In my quieter moments, I still miss it. It wasn't just the fun and the camaraderie – I'll admit I liked the attention of having the band and a bit of a regular following in the area. Mostly though, I simply enjoyed the company of the lads. They were a good bunch and we had become great mates. I reckon every last one of them now regrets behaving like a mule. If you actually asked them now what it was they were fighting over, they probably wouldn't know.

Maybe it went back a long time, like I said. Maybe it's just how bands are. Maybe it's how the Poles are in that terrible climate – passionate yet unpredictable, fighting against the knowledge that nothing good will ever last and eventually losing hope. Whatever it was, I wasn't able to understand it. But it upset me a lot. It also upset Janusz to an awful degree. In fact, I was as sorry for him as I was for myself. Even if all we did for him was rekindle some fond memories from days gone by, that was something.

The end of the club and the end of that band meant an end to another chapter for me. You close it and move on and there's no point getting too sentimental about it. I'm a nostalgic bugger though. Coming over to a foreign country and getting that close to people is a hard thing to forget, especially as it finished on a bum note. Something else comes along and eventually these things maintain a distance, but they're never really that far away in the mind. You are always going to miss them.

I stayed in touch with Jarek for some time afterwards, but saw little of the rest of them. Kazik got married and had a kid and one night I arranged to meet him. I remember the night well. A blizzard was raging outside and temperatures were heading for minus fifteen. He called into me and we went to his house together, a small but cozy rented cottage a little way out of town. On the way, he asked if he could borrow money. His wife was visiting her mother with the kid and wouldn't be home until the next day, but he had no coal to heat the house for them. I gladly loaned him some money, as he was an incredibly reliable chap, and we bought a few beers and a few bags of coal.

When we got to the house the cold was truly unbearable. It was so cold that it was almost painful just sitting there. I had thought that I was used to it by then. Kazik had vodka, which of course gives the impression of warmth, and we drank that until the boiler was fired. We had a good chat then, drank a few beers and more vodka and he played me a tape of the band. One that he had recorded at a gig. Every now and again, he would jump forward on the seat, clenching imaginary drumsticks and shouting, 'Remember this bit, Tom! Remember! Dah-na-nah dum! Super.'

Three Colours White

When APSO brought all of us together for a meeting in the monastery at the end of the fourth year, those who were still in the country as teachers knew what was coming. The project was over. That was that. Four years, they had decided, was enough. It was a sensible thing to do. It was obvious that Poland would very soon emerge as a strong contender for EU membership – in fact, it would only be five years away. It did mean, however, that I would be staying in the country for another year without the support of APSO, living only on a Polish salary, which had not increased all that much. When I came back from the meeting and told Asha what the decision was, we had a joint panic.

There were a few of us holding out for another year, some simply because it had become a reliable job, in a country we had got used to and with long holidays and freedom to boot. I, however, needed the last year to wait for Asha to finish her studies. But at least I had the accommodation, as long as I chose to stay with the school on their terms and if the school still needed me. They did, but we had to pull a lot of strokes to get the Department of Education to agree, and to get the right documents for a resident permit. All that had been a matter of course when there was cooperation between the two governments. Once that was cut off, a lot of red tape appeared. The school director worked tirelessly to secure me another year there.

I had become worn out from teaching though. I can't quite put my finger on any single event that caused such aversion to something that I had always wanted to do. It was really a combination of several factors that layered up, particularly in the final year. For one, I began to doubt my ability as a teacher. I might have been a reasonably good one initially and my heart was at least in it. But I had lost interest and really had a duty to the students to call it a day. Without the support of APSO, there was also a feeling of isolation, of abandonment, a feeling that the sense of purpose was now gone.

I began to notice something else that went deeper than any of that. I was no longer the new kid in town. I was older. I was going to be thirty. I had actually become a teacher, the asshole that comes around the corner every morning and makes the kids groan.

It's some knock back when things get to that stage. When the new kids in school began calling me 'sir' or 'professor' instead of 'Tom', as I had always been called, I had to have a long, hard think. Vanity. It gets you every time.

Losing the lads in the band as close friends was something else that I found very hard to cope with. It was great to have such ties with Polish people, and while there were plenty of others that I had become close to, it wasn't the same. The guys had been real buddies and my social life – apart from the odd weekend in Warsaw where the remainder of my Irish friends were – had been non-existent without their company in the last year. I missed that more than I thought I would.

In the final year, I found myself increasingly bored and restless. I went on the beer on the weekends with whoever would come along, purely to kill time, while Asha, studying for her final exams, stuck her head in the books at any opportunity. I was glad she was doing that. She was a real grafter, but it was a long year with very, very little of any consequence happening, other than our engagement in the spring. That delighted Asha's mother, who, God bless her, was probably terrified that I was going to do a runner, even if Asha and I had taken it for granted from the moment I looked into her eyes before devouring the roast chicken on that first night, long, long ago.

Sadly, Asha's father had died early in my third year there, and it was a great pity that he was not going to be around for his first daughter's wedding. Although he spoke no English, we had always managed to enjoy family gatherings when he was present. He was a very lively and kindly old soul, who had helped me get a bank loan for the stereo. That stereo, as you can imagine, was a Godsend, as I had up to that point only had a tape player.

It might seem strange citing that memory, but if he helped a stranger by guaranteeing a loan for him, I'd like to believe there was enough trust there for him to approve of my marrying his daughter. I'm sure there was, but I often thought that I needed some sign of approval, and wondered if it would ever come.

One summer evening, the wedding only weeks away, there was a knock on my door. I opened it to see the director of the boarding block, who told me that there was a foreigner downstairs. He had arrived in Minsk and had been directed to the internat for accommodation as, of course, there was no hotel in the town. Did I want to meet him, she asked.

I was completely taken by surprise, as ridiculous as that sounds. I had discovered, some time ago, that there was another foreigner in the town, a Scottish man, who lived across the railway track and taught in the mechanical school. In five years, I never saw the guy. He must have known about my existence too, but he never sought me out. As to why, I can't say. Maybe the fear of having to meet regularly after an introduction was too great in such a small town. I really don't know.

So, do I want to meet this other new impostor? I shrug, and before I have a chance to answer the director, this guy comes up the stairs and gives me a wave. A small, fit-looking fella with long hair and a friendly smile, he introduces himself as Howard from Australia, and, just like an Aussie, in he comes.

He enters the hallway, looking around with a craned neck, then into my main room, which at this point is full of all kinds of stuff, as I had travelled quite a bit in the last few years.

'So this is where it all happens,' he says with a smile.

'Yeah. So what the hell are you doing here?' I ask him. 'This is the first time I've ever met another foreigner in this place.'

'Jesus, mate, I should be asking you that. How long are you here?'

'Five years.'

'Five years!' he says with a startled laugh. 'What have you been doing here for five years?'

I explain to Howard, who is on a solo cycling trip around Eastern Europe and has found himself in Minsk by mistake, that he has entered my story at the final chapter, and is welcome to hang around for a few days to see it come to a close. That evening, I tell him, I have to meet the local priest to officially register for a marriage course. He looks at me, the smile getting wider, the incredulity carved onto his face.

By way of explanation, I take him over to Asha's flat and the three of us go to the restaurant in the local cultural building, where he tries to get vegetarian food. Not a hope. From there we go to the local church and he waits around outside while we go in to meet the priest.

When we came out, the smile was still on Howard's face, and I swear the guy kept that smile for the three days he spent in the internat resting. He accompanied myself and Asha everywhere for those few days as we tied up all the loose ends and prepared for the official side of marriage. In the evenings we'd go for a quiet beer and a chat, the three of us. It was one of those chance but wonderful meetings, where someone crosses your path so unexpectedly, you love their company, and then they're gone. I don't know which of us was more amused – me for having suddenly met another foreigner after all this time, or him for having come across a guy living in this middle-of-nowhere town, going to the local church to attend marriage courses.

After his three days of recuperation, he got up early one morning and left, and that was the end of him. For a while, Asha and I used to joke about the Aussie who had blown into town and become so intimate with our wedding plans, even though he was a total stranger. I believed I would never hear from him again, but about a year later, I got a letter from Howard at my parents' address, which I had given him. In it he wrote that stumbling upon myself and Asha was one of the more memorable events of his trip across Eastern Europe. He added that he was convinced we were a couple who were made for each other, and wished us both luck and success for the rest of our lives.

It was a lovely letter, like a seal of approval from someone who had just dropped in for that short but very important time, then vanished again. I lost the letter, so I never got to write back to him. But sometimes these incidents are meant to be fleeting.

A few weeks after Howard left, our wedding day was upon us. I had completed the courses, at which I met several of my students. One of the speakers, a woman who worked as a counsellor, had informed all present that a marriage between an older woman and a younger man will never work, and a marriage between two people of different nationalities will never work either. At the end of the evening I went up with Asha and told her that I was a foreigner. Did we have any chance? 'No,' she said, adding, 'I'm right.' I remember little from those marriage courses apart from that, so I was determined to prove the auld bitch wrong.

The priest, a man probably younger than myself, was more endearing. Following the course, all the couples had to pass a test in the church with the priest – reciting various prayers, refuting Satan, that sort of thing. I just nodded away and managed to scrape a pass. God forbid you would stumble at that stage. But between the courses, the tests and that old tramp of a counsellor, I was a bundle of nerves the night before my wedding.

The weather during the build-up hadn't helped either, as far as ensuring sleep and a half-decent complexion for the relatives. The town had been basking in temperatures that soared into the thirties and, with no breeze at night, there was no respite from the heat. Sleep just wouldn't come. We were plagued by mosquitoes that year and with no air-conditioning, had to leave the windows open. There was no defence from the onslaught of those whiny little bastards. Actually, they were pretty big whiny bastards in Poland, as I recall, and their bites hurt. Someone told me later though, that there was a radio station in Warsaw called Radio Z, which if left on at night keeps the mosquitoes away. That bad, I wondered? No, it broadcasted on the same frequency as a bat's signal, apparently. Since bats fed on mosquitoes, mosquitoes wouldn't enter a room if they believed there were bats in there. I found that a bit of a stretch myself, but I would have tried it nonetheless, if I'd known.

Several of Asha's cousins arrived the night before the wedding and were staying in the internat block, which at this point in the summer was empty of students. One had left a case of beer at the door of my flat. I resisted the temptation to drink the whole thing, but the next morning there was a bang on my door, followed by a raucous request to open up. It was Asha's cousin Robert, a great big friendly fella, who barged in and began cracking open beers, insisting it was a custom to do so on the morning of a wedding. In his hand was a packet of what looked like crisps, which we ate heartily to accompany the beer. It was actually pigs' ears from Lithuania, where he had come from himself. That was enough. I turfed him out, sat in a cold bath for half an hour, then pulled myself into a suit to go and meet the bus that was coming from Warsaw with family and friends.

A Polish wedding begins in the home of the bride, where parents of both sides gather to wish the couple a successful marriage and have a small toast. It's a nice, intimate way of starting the day and, unlike in Ireland, you get to see the bride one last time before you marry.

Outside Asha's flat, there was a lump in my throat watching all my close friends and family clambering off the bus and staring about them in wonderment. Five years, ye hoors, and you finally come over in such numbers when I've to pay for a wedding. A violin and an accordion player livened the atmosphere with Gypsy music. Heads appeared at every window of the block of flats to watch as our procession made its way up the road to the church.

If you can put nerves onto a scale, getting married would definitely be close to the top, somewhere between execution and root canal treatment. But standing there as people slowly made their way into the cool of the building, with a solitary violin playing the sweetest music I have ever heard, I don't think I have ever known a happier moment.

Like all Polish weddings, it was a long, festive day, made even more special by the amount of people who had come over from home. We had the reception in an army barracks of all places, since in this country weddings, New Year parties or debs balls are all held in whatever buildings are available in the town. It could be an airport hangar or a factory, but you would never know once inside, as a lot of work goes into decorating them.

If memory serves me right, there were about 150 guests, 150 bottles of vodka, fifty bottles of wine and a few kegs of beer. Food was served continuously through-out the night – pork, salads made from all the usual sus-pects, herring, tatar, all present. It ended with boiled sausages at 4am. While commenting on the food in Poland, though, the dish that dealt the greatest jolt of astonishment among the Irish guests was the one that had floored me the first year – Zurek, the soup with the boiled egg. They had been served it in a restaurant in Warsaw on their first night, and talked about it continuously until they got on the plane for home. The egg in the soup.

Of course, I eventually grew to understand the import Poles place on the humble egg and how strongly it features in Polish culture. It is a wholesome and potent symbol of life and the universe, of the sun and of rebirth. At Easter it is dyed in many colours, placed in baskets and blessed. You see kids with their families walking with baskets of painted eggs up to the church and it is a tremendous sight. The painting of the eggs supposedly comes from a legend that Mary, while at the cross, gave eggs to the soldiers, requesting them to be less cruel. When she wept, the tears falling on the eggs resulted in a rainbow of colours. Well and good. As to why it went into the soup, I never really discovered. It probably just hap-pened to be there, so in it went.

The reception went on until 5.30am, at which time, I'm ashamed to say, I was found sitting with the band members, drinking the vodka that had been in such abundance. It was their fault. One of Asha's friends had to help me into a car to go back to my boarding house where I lay, in a drunken diagonal, from one corner of the bed to the other, leaving a triangle wedge for my new wife. I didn't get breakfast in bed. But we'd had a day to remember. We were both exhausted and emotionally, well, I was overwhelmed.

The thrill of being married was followed by a hard landing within a week, upon coming back from a trip to southern Poland with some of the Irish guests. We had really organised nothing, not even knowing where we would live – at my school flat or in Asha's flat, which would mean having no privacy at all. We tried a bit of both, and neither worked. Asha didn't want to live in a school boarding block and I went stir crazy living in a flat with Asha's mother and sister. After years of independence, I couldn't do it. People had even asked me how I was going to manage living with a wife suddenly after all that time. Most people practise for about a year before taking the plunge. Faith, love, hope and charity was the answer I had for that one. But they weren't going to get us out of the hole we were then in.

We had loosely agreed to continue doing what we were doing, but with the festivities over, the guests returned home and the future staring us in the face, things looked different. There weren't any real job prospects in Poland for myself, apart from teaching. So I tried one other route that I thought might work.

Towards the end of that fifth year, myself and Barry dreamed up the notion of creating our own magazine for the ex-pats of Warsaw. It seemed rash, but actually, unlike owning our own bar, it was more feasible given the right amount of work, a book of contacts and good intuition. The first two of these were there; I think it was the third part that let us down in the end.

We had several guys around Warsaw who were working for the *Warsaw Voice* and were happy to contribute. We had people in a few businesses who were available for support and ready to throw ads at us. And finally, we met an Englishman one night who was willing to invest if he thought the project was interesting enough. So we got a rough plan together and went to meet him. It was only then that the depth of our ignorance became evident.

This man was what people term a venture, or 'vulture', capitalist. A very helpful character nonetheless, he met us one evening in one of Warsaw's top hotels and we explained as best we could what our masterplan was. He seemed reasonably impressed until he asked us how much money we were looking for to start up. This was something we'd been discussing for weeks. Do we go for the big one and ask for a million, or do we look at a small figure that will get us off the ground? We decided on the latter and when we mentioned a sum of five or ten grand, he slammed his folder shut and sat back, shaking his head. We began whimpering, changing our figure to three grand, two grand, but his head continued to shake.

'You don't understand, guys, if you'd asked me for half a million, a million, I'd have obliged. You're sitting here giving me names of a few hacks in the *Warsaw Voice,* you should be telling me you want to buy the *Warsaw Voice.*'

Sometimes reality has a harsh bite and we felt the teeth marks for weeks after that. The man was right. Why invest ten grand to get eleven grand back, when you can invest a million and get back two? And why didn't that occur to us? Where had we been the last five years? That demon had come to haunt us. We had been stagnating in small rural towns for so long, we'd forgotten that the rest of the world was rapidly passing us by. That included Warsaw. There were many people like this Englishman, over to invest in the new market.

Poles were leaving their villages and small towns in droves, coming up to the capital to take advantage of the influx of foreign companies into the city. Those companies wouldn't have been there if it were never going to prove financially viable. The problem with involving yourself in a country that is 'in transition', is that you yourself are at great risk of standing still.

So we decided, Asha and I, literally within the week, to leave. We went into the tourist office on a Friday and bought a one-way ticket out for the following week. It was a quick decision and an easy one to make. Whatever reason I had for coming here five years ago, there was no reason for my being here any longer. Even the school director, a great man who had done so much for me over the years, knew it. Unlike every other year, he didn't even try to persuade me to stay any longer. He thanked me, gave me a presentation at a teachers' meeting and it was all over. It was very abrupt, but it was probably best that way.

Despite this, I admit to being pretty despondent at the prospect of leaving for good. The first year, although it was the toughest and loneliest year of my life, was also the most enjoyable and emotional year I will probably ever have. The teachers in the school were beautiful, warm people, as were ninety percent of the kids. At the end of each school year, when a group of classes finished their Matura and left, my heart would sink knowing that I'd never see them again.

There were many students that I grew close to, who I think about in my quieter moments, and who I hope have found good lives for themselves. If it wasn't for them – their resilience, their openness and the sheer warmth they had for me – I'm sure I would very quickly have just left. The group I came over with were also incredible, and even if we didn't get to meet up as much as we should have, some have become lifelong friends.

It wasn't conquering the Himalayas. It wasn't saving lives in Bosnia. It was probably selfishness rather than altruism that drove me there in the first place. But it was good. There was also something of a paradox in it: The longer I stayed, the further away from that first, incredible year I grew. It was the benchmark by which I measured everything. It is a hard thing to look back at a peak, regardless of what stage you are at in your life, knowing that it, or anything like it, is never to be repeated. It is also a little strange calling what must sound like abject misery a peak.

I often wondered if our project achieved anything. The simple answer is, I don't know. It is one thing to feel you've achieved something on a personal level – matured, learned more about yourself, humanity and living – but it is a different thing to attempt to gauge your broader success. I know there were those who were grateful, but gratitude is no real measure of accomplishment. I was sure, however, that the country was a long way from resolving its problems and was about to face new and inescapable ones.

Shortly before I was due to leave, I had a visit from one of my old students. She was a fabulous girl and had achieved a '6' grade, almost unheard of, in her English Matura. She called to my flat and asked me how she could get to London to work for the summer. I told her that, as it was already the end of June, there wasn't much chance. She seemed almost desperate, saying that I was her only hope – which was a bit desperate – and that she badly needed to work abroad over the summer to make money for the following year in college. I went over the various official courses of action and finally outlined the other route – hopping on a plane or bus and hoping for the best.

But I had already seen countless men, women and students turned back from the airport, or, once when I got a bus to London, at the ports. There was one man I remember in particular, who, having travelled almost forty hours on the bus to visit his daughter in England, was put on a bus straight back to Poland, heartbroken. It was tough for Poles. This girl knew that was a risk that would incur serious loss if she failed. I don't know what she decided to do in the end, and I was sorry I couldn't help her. I felt I owed them all something. At the same time, I knew that freedom to move across Europe was not too far away, and that there was a chance that she, and others I had taught over the years, would one day stroll around Dublin, free to look for a job and make some decent money.

Packing after such a length of time is a strange thing. As you drag the items together one by one, there's a sense of finality about it. It's not just a wash bag and a few books. There are things that suggest permanency and have a strong scent of the place that for so long was called home, things that are inevitably left until last. And there's a lump in your throat as you go through them all – birthday cards, Christmas cards, withered flowers, empty bottles, drawings from the kids in school, old exercise books, obsolete money with strings of zeros and pictures of communists.

There are bits of furniture that have accumulated over the years. There's the beast of a Polish television that took up a whole corner. There's the brown, rectangular radio from the 1950s that the director gave me as company in the first week. There's a rug whose colour has faded from years of sun, snow, muck and sand on the soles of boots. There are tins of food that were never eaten. Newspapers under the spare bed. Bottles under the sink. Clothes that were never worn.

These are the things you can't take with you. So they go into large black bags and then into the skip. Then there's the photo-frame. Pictures of students, teachers, the band, great Polish friends who I haven't seen for so long and are probably married and have kids. Every photo has a story, a moment. Each face frozen in a place in time that is as clear now as when it first happened. I won't get to say goodbye to any of them.

The photos just made that lump more prominent and I went to bed feeling just like a stranger should feel leaving a strange land, only I was no longer really a stranger. Lying there, I began to go over the images I'd conjured up for myself before arriving, comparing them to what I'd seen so far. You don't expect a thousand volts of culture shock coming to a place like this. It's not the centre of Africa or the Middle East. It's still Europe, but it's a part of Europe that most of us have only peeped at while it was hidden behind the iron curtain.

The timber houses, smoke gasping out of their chimneys day and night, sitting under the shadow of grey blocks that clawed the landscape like broken umbrellas.

Old men with shattered teeth, young girls with bright blonde hair, packed under scarves decorated with the flowers of spring. Fields that were golden in autumn and steel blue in winter. Cold vodka, warm beds and the sound of men singing in taverns, keeping a beat with the thud of beer tankards on long wooden tables. Then I just drifted off to sleep. Only this time not alone.

Afterword

May 2005. Sunday, 2pm. Outside St Michan's Church in Smithfield, Dublin, crowds of Poles begin to gather.

There are cars and vans with Polish registrations. There are new arrivals eating Polish food from backpacks. There is even a man selling Polish newspapers: *Gazeta Wyborcza*, the paper of the electorate, with over five million readers, which began as a humble eight-page weekly in May 1989, published by some of those who had previously published an underground paper; and *Tygodnik Mazowsze* (meaning The Weekly Mazowiecki, after the region in Poland).

'How much for the paper?'

'Two euro,' he says.

'But it says two zloty on the cover.'

'A zloty for a euro,' he smiles.

Actually it's not. There are four zloty to a euro. But he's right to be charging more. The papers had to be taken all the way overland from Warsaw by bus, a bus operated from a Polish office in Store Street in Dublin, which arrives twice weekly, full of Poles, to be met by more Poles. Some are picking up parcels sent by their families back home, others who were unsuccessful at finding a job are climbing back on board. For the time being, that bus and the newspapers it brings are the only source of income for this man, who has been here three weeks, with little money and no English.

Work is all he talks about, until his colleague tells him that mass is about to start. Within minutes, the whole crowd outside is jammed inside and you wouldn't fit a mass leaflet between the bodies.

Fr Andrew Pyka, who says mass at St Michan's, arrived here in 2003 as Parish Priest of Sallynoggin, having worked in Australia for twenty years and England for five. Before Poland acceded to the EU, a Polish mass was an occasional feature in the calendar of the Polish-Irish Society in Fitzwilliam Square, celebrated if there happened to be a Polish priest here for study leave or even just for a visit. May 2004 changed all that. By November of that year, 50,000 immigrants from the ten new EU states arrived in Ireland, almost 25,000 of them Poles. And these were only figures collated at the time from the PPSN (Personal Public Service Numbers) data, which only counts registered workers.

'Fitzwilliam was just inadequate,' says Fr Andrew. 'There were more services needed. People were standing all over the place and even to have a cup of tea it was impossible. I was hearing confessions in the toilets because there was no room.'

Confession? There was really such a demand for confession?

'Poles won't go to communion without going to confession. And there are marriage preparation courses to do too. Okay, we've got the equivalent here, but some of them couldn't cope with the language barrier. Generally, ninety-five percent are Polish people marrying Polish people. And there is going to be more and more. In January I finished courses for some fifty couples. And there will be another one in April.

'But that's only one part of it. There are constant requests from people from places like Belfast. Some come to Sallynoggin on the bus just for confessions. I'm going to New Ross and the Wexford area to hear mass. On Easter Monday I'm going to Limerick, because there is no one there. There is no one in Cork. I'm getting requests from there. Plus I have my own parish here, with 2,500 families. I can't let them down.'

In 2005, Fr Andrew was still the sole representative of the Polish Catholic Church in Ireland. He managed to get the use of St Michan's after discussions with Archbishop Diarmuid Martin. But very quickly, even this church became inadequate. Apart from the masses, he badly needed to improve on the social area upstairs where the congregation were invited to meet after mass. It was just too small for socialising.

'So if they want to go and socialise they go to the pub,' he says. 'And they drink like hell and they get drunk. And then they fight.'

This worries him. He told the Archbishop that he was

sitting on a 'pastoral bomb' that might explode. There are other ethnic groups in the city – Lithuanians, Russians, Ukranians – who 'were not such good pals when we were in Poland and they were behind the border because they were part of Russia'. If frustration, financial difficulties and all the problems that go with emigration are not channeled through him, the only familiar voice in a foreign country, then how might thousands vent their dissatisfaction?

There are plenty of Polish people in Ireland who have professional careers. There are plenty of students who will come over, assimilate and vanish into the crowds. Fr Pyka's problem is that most Polish people here are 'working within the 1000-word group' and won't cope with integration that easily.

'Remember the reason they are coming here is to send some bacon home. It is so sad when some of them get lost completely. And that worries me. In Poland – I don't want to say simple people – but ordinary people in towns and villages, everybody goes to the church. You remove them from that environment and they can't find their feet. They get lost.

'Faith was what helped us to survive for so long. And if you take the faith from the Polish people they haven't got much. Faith is very closely linked with our nationality. You wouldn't expect to meet a Polish person who is not a Catholic. Because of our faith we were able to stay together and fight back.'

A week later I return to the same church at the same time. A man gives me a slip of paper with a number on it and asks if I need a lift to Poland. He works as a refrigeration technician for an Irish company who have given him a company car. He doesn't need his own car, so he'll drive it back home to his family. But why travel in an empty car? He can fill the seats with people and make some money.

Another man, in his early fifties, a tiler from Bydgoscszc. He has no English whatsover and is struggling to find a job. He borrowed from a bank to get here and his family is waiting at home for money. He asks about me, my wife and whether I have children. When I tell him I've no children because they're too expensive and I needed a house first, he's shocked. Rent a house, he says. Family is more important than houses. Maybe, but he doesn't know modern Ireland.

The man with the newspapers is there again. Only they are the same newspapers that he was selling last week. He shrugs and blames the bus, which had no room for newspapers this week. It was too full of people. Just like the mass.

Two years later, the Polish community in Ireland has mushroomed. Everybody talks about them. There are Polish programmes on an Irish television channel, articles appearing in papers about professional Poles, presumably as opposed to the tradesmen, the Polish plumbers. There are Polish newspapers, like the *Polski Herald*, printed by an Irish newspaper. And there are papers printed by Poles for Poles. There are Polish shops in Dublin, Limerick, Cork, Newry and elsewhere, shops where many of the staff don't even speak English.

There are road safety campaigns and government information leaflets translated into Polish and any bank with an ounce of sense employs as many Polish people as they can get in their doors.

There are up to six Polish teams playing football in Dublin alone, in the Brian Kerr anti-racism league, and there are regular gigs by visiting Polish bands who have also seen the market in Ireland's new immigrants.

The low-cost airlines are adding routes to various parts of Poland so fast that Dublin airport can't keep up. And the buses are arriving several times a week now, offloading a couple of hundred more Poles. With their Polish papers and their bags of cabbage and sausage, they disappear down the quays somewhere in the dark.

Fr Pyka's campaign to get a new church and more helpers even paid off. Fr Jaroslaw Maszkiewicz is the new chaplain in Ireland, and Archbishop Diarmuid Martin presented the Poles with their own new church, St Audeon's on High Street, with an inaugural mass attended by the Polish primate, Cardinal Jozef Glemp, in September 2006. But you can count on Poles to get things done, that's for certain. At the mass, Cardinal Glemp said that, 'I believe Ireland will become the place of return to faith for many of you and will deepen the bond with your Homeland.' A 'return' to faith sounds like an unusual comment. Judging by the amount of Polish masses, from Abbeyfeale to Youghal, now listed on the Polish chaplaincy website, there is no shortage of Poles attending church here. It is the Irish who have lost their faith.

One of the other leading Polish newspapers, *Rzeczpospolita*, conducted a poll asking people whether they were going to go abroad for work in 2007. 'Yes,' was the answer given by twelve percent of those questioned. That's about 3.2 million citizens and only three countries are likely to be chosen as a destination – Germany, the UK and Ireland. According to the paper, in 2006 about 360,000 Poles had already gone abroad for work.

Even the Polish president, Lech Kacynski, who bragged about unemployment coming down from almost twenty percent – forgetting that 360,000 of the labour force had left – couldn't resist the lure of the Emerald Isle. Having taunted those who went abroad and left their motherland to seek work, in February 2007 he paid a state visit to Ireland to praise them. He also managed to put his community at risk of serious reprimand, if not worse, by saying that logically – and, of course, biologically – the human race would disappear eventually if homosexuality were to become the dominant sexual persuasion. He was ambushed into saying that by someone who was aware that his government didn't exactly keep a check on the 'gay bashers' who attack Gay Pride marches. And his government have done a lot more to bring down the wrath of the EU upon them. But, as any Pole will tell you, there are a lot worse than the Kaczynski twins when it comes to right-wing politics in Poland.

There are problems now in the construction industry in Poland. People who buy a new apartment buy it 'in the raw' – an empty shell. Skirting, sinks, partition walls, bathrooms, the whole shebang has to be sourced. They need to find the plumbers, the carpenters and the plasterers to complete their new homes. But there are none to be found. If you do find one, be prepared to wait. And to pay for it.

Polish service industries have had to look to countries like the Ukraine to fill jobs in the hotels and bars. And who is going to pick the fruit in summer that is so vital to Poland's economy? The Moldovans maybe?

But we could be looking at our own problems soon. Dell in Limerick is the most efficient Dell plant in the world. It is also the lifeblood of Limerick, with 3,000 employed. In fact, six in every 100 workers in the Limerick, Clare and west Tipperary region work for Dell. And where are Dell planning to go to? Poland. Procter and Gamble have been employing 280 people since 1985 in Nenagh, but in a cost-cutting measure they're packing up shop. Where are they going? Poland.

Is this the start of a trend? One wonders, did the Irish government not have a plan when they opened their borders? Did they not see that before its entry into the EU in 2004, Poland cut its corporate tax rate from twenty-seven percent to nineteen percent? The corporate tax rate in Ireland is still a low 12.5% for trading income. But factories that move to Poland can find workers who will be happy to toil for €300 a month. Throw in cheaper property prices and better infrastructure in the large pool of cities available, and one wonders how long we will be hanging onto our new Polish friends.

Another question. How many Poles do we include among our group of friends, even giving the term 'friend' a bit of latitude when it comes to definition? Of course, you will find the few Poles from the office going for pints after work on Friday night. But did many Irish people invite Poles into their homes over Christmas or Easter, the way we were invited that first year when many of us were lost, lonely and half-starved in poor towns in eastern Poland? You will find these issues discussed on a website for the Polish community here. The Irish are great to go out and get drunk with, but I still haven't been asked around to their houses, said one blogger.

Of course, nobody really wants that many new friends. New friends can be a pain in the arse.

'That's the second time we were out for dinner with the Polish neighbours. Do you think we have to ask them over to the barbie next Sunday?'

'Christ, no. I mean, we'll have your friends from work and a few of the guys are coming over – it will be a bit awkward. We'll give them a shout again.'

The most interesting aspect of working on the Polish paper at the *Herald* was the reaction to it from Irish people. Calls constantly came in from potential advertisers, who would tell you how many Poles there are in Ireland and how huge a market it has become. You had callers who owned this or that bar or restaurant or club, who were sure the Poles would love to come along. For most of them, the Poles were 'a market'.

Not everyone thought that way though, not by any means. The Augustinian Friars in Smithfield in Dublin fed queues of unfortunate Poles daily. There were countless other charities that would phone out of genuine concern. You would get Irish people representing sporting clubs, societies and other bodies who, in another genuine gesture, wanted to place notices inviting Poles to join their respective groups in a social capacity. Then you had the old faithfuls.

'I'm ringing a second time to complain about that Polish Herald blocking up my dustbin,' says the woman on the phone, without so much as an introduction. 'Is that the Polish Herald?'

'It is,' I reply. 'What's the problem exactly?'

'That Polish paper, it's a disgrace so it is. I don't want it in the paper that I've been buying for years. Why can't they do their own paper? It's a disgrace, having to look at that every week.'

'Well, it's a supplement,' I say. 'You can just pull it out.'

'And why should I have to pay bin charges to get that rubbish taken away? It's a disgrace so it is. Why don't you have an Irish paper?'

'Well, the rest of the paper *is* an Irish paper.'

'Irish language, I'm talking about.'

'I suppose there's no real demand for it. I mean, what exactly is your problem with the *Polski Herald*? It's only twelve pages.'

'They should get their own paper and leave our paper alone.'

'Well, it would be too expensive just to print a separate twelve-page paper.'

'Charge them then. Charge them twelve pence!'

Dear, oh dear. Apparently, the guys on the front desk frequently get calls of that nature. And in one sense, you can understand it. It's not that it's hard to tear out this offensive supplement, it's the fact that it is there in the first place. It's like seeing a thistle one morning in your bed of daffodils. How did it get there? You can dig it up, but the damage has been done. The scene has been spoiled, the memory has been trounced upon and nothing will ever be the same again.

It leads you to wonder that while on the whole, the reception for Poles in Ireland has been good, at what point will the picture begin to change? Shops, papers, hairdressers and bars. That's allowed. They can work as waiters, construction workers and kitchen porters. That's allowed. We can continue to treat them as a market and tell each other how great it is. But what about when the real success stories begin to happen? What about success-ful Polish businesses? What happens when the Irish begin working for the Poles? What happens when the Irish have to pay rent to a Polish landlord? And what happens when more and more jobs are lost as factories and multinationals head off to Polska, while the Poles are cleaning up over here?

I met two Polish students in Warsaw who had spent time in Ireland, with mixed experiences. They were treated well in work – they both worked as waitresses and bar staff and were paid up to €12 an hour, almost twice the minimum wage. And they were very fond of the Irish people who they socialised and worked with.

They had met with some intimidating situations on the street, however, and one recalled that friends had been turned away from a central-Dublin pub with the remark that they had 'fucking Polish faces'. They had horror stories of living ten to a room and of encountering Polish criminals on the streets who now had a free run from East to West. We have already had plenty of instances of Poles committing crimes here. I know the type, Poles know the type, and they are not the type we want. But who knows the difference when there are no checks?

These two students had a story about friends being beaten up by guys with golf clubs, and they had stories about girls being beaten up by Irish girls, who were more ferocious than the Irish guys, in their estimation.

They complained about life in Poland, how tough it was to make ends meet and to buy an apartment, and how their parents, who held very good jobs, were only earning €200 a month. They despaired at the amount of

Irish swooping in and scooping up properties with both fists. As regards the foreseeable future in Poland, they couldn't see one.

Other than those with wanderlust, most of the Poles in this country, if people had occasion to hear their stories, don't really want to be here at all. While they are, most just want to keep their heads down and get on with life, the same as the rest of us.

It is easy for the media to lump the Poles into one large slice of the immigrant pie chart. Commentators in newspapers have differing opinions on the whole 'immigrant question', some taking the view that Ireland is such a dull old place that it's great for new cultures to come in and brighten it up a bit.

That attitude is a reasonably noble one, but neglects the fact that probably the majority of immigrants – Polish or otherwise – aren't interested in integrating or mixing with the natives either. They are here to fulfil a purpose and are, just like so many Irish in England, Australia and the US, happy to live, work and hang out with their own kind. The new shops that sell those mad-looking sausages are not there to benefit the Irish, but the Poles. And judging by the amount of these shops, hairdressers and so on, many of them couldn't be arsed with integration.

Ask any teacher in a primary school what it's like trying to cope with a class of kids with mixed nationalities, and they'll probably say that as well as having familiarity classes for teachers to understand the sensitivities of others, the kids and the parents of these kids should be learning about Irish culture and the English language before they arrive, and for a period while they settle. It works both ways or it doesn't work at all.

Personally, I like having so many Poles over here. It reminds me of home.